S0-BJH-121

DATE DUE

MY 16 '80	JUL 23 1985	NOV 7 - 1991
NOV 2 5 1981		NOV 0 4 2010
	JUL 2 6 1990	

743.936   34579
B141L   Baer, Curtis
         Landscape drawings

RENNER
LEARNING RESOURCES
CENTER
ELGIN COMMUNITY COLLEGE
ELGIN, ILLINOIS

DEMCO

LANDSCAPE DRAWINGS

TO HELMUTH LÜTJENS

LANDSCAPE DRAWINGS

Curtis O. Baer

743.936
B141L

RENNER LEARNING RESOURCES CENTER
ELGIN COMMUNITY COLLEGE
ELGIN, ILLINOIS

Published in association with the Drawing Society

HARRY N. ABRAMS, INC., PUBLISHERS   NEW YORK

Frontispiece: Vincent Van Gogh,
Fields and Farmhouses near Arles (see p. 326)

Book design by Robin Fox

H. F. Cary's translation of Dante's *The Divine Comedy*
used by permission of E. P. Dutton & Co., Inc.

Standard Book Number: 8109-0255-9
Library of Congress Catalogue Card Number: 77-135655
All rights reserved. No part of the contents of this book may be
reproduced without the written permission of the publishers
Harry N. Abrams, Incorporated, New York, N. Y.

Printed and bound in Japan

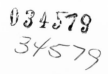

034579
34579

CONTENTS

When Winslow Ames asked me to write the volume on landscape in a series planned by the Drawing Society, I knew at once that nothing could appeal to me more. It was an opportunity not to be passed up, the more so as a comprehensive study of landscape drawings never had been made (since then Agnes Mongan's superb essay has appeared in *Daedalus,* 1963).

Not that this book is the missing history of landscape drawings. It is an anthology; the illustrations are the central feature. They are to show the many facets of Western landscape, as well as the direction of its development. An anthology can present only a tiny fraction of the material; the task was to select examples that are representative, diversified, and of high quality.

There were the usual dilemmas: whether to concentrate on the great masters or to display a larger variety; which artists and which of their products to choose. But such problems never were really perplexing. In case of doubt, I gave preference to an attractive piece over a typical one.

Some examples have been included which, by strict standards, are not landscapes. I was not guided by the rule of one museum where landscape is defined as "a painting, drawing, or print in which at least forty percent of the surface represents vegetative matter." When the general character of a sheet was based on nature or on the relation of nature to man, I felt free to call it a landscape, even if figures or buildings were dominant. The selection is equally unorthodox in what is considered a drawing. Sometimes an artist could be documented better by a watercolor than in black and white.

To gather these 160 examples was sheer pleasure. It provided all the excitement of collecting, but without being hemmed in by prices and availability—a collector's wildest and fondest dream. Naturally, the selection reflects my own preferences. The expert in a special period will spot the shortcomings instantly.

The notes to the illustrations are intended to supply factual information as well as the reason why a particular drawing appealed to me. I hope that some of my enthusiasm has spilled over into the comments. They also attempt to place the examples in their historical context, to give a connecting story of sorts. The bibliographical references are kept to a minimum, except in cases where recent scholarly findings seemed important. Owing to the lapse of time between finishing the manuscript and its publication, references to the latest literature are missing.

The Introduction tries to outline some basic concepts of Western landscape and of its development. The approach may seem too personal, the opinions may appear arbitrary and hard to prove. Writing on aesthetic experiences is a precarious undertaking. Max J. Friedländer mentioned that it always sounds like a bad translation. Yet anyone who, in front of a work of art, has tried to transform his strong but vague sensations into language, knows that such an attempt is not only difficult and often frustrating but also rewarding.

I have received assistance and advice from so many scholars that it is impossible to repeat my thanks individually. In particular, I wish to express my gratitude to Mlle. Roseline Bacou, Miss A. H. Scott-Elliot, Mr. Frits Lugt, Mr. Carlos van Hasselt, Mr. John Gere, Dr. Eckhart Knab, and Dr. Matthias Winner. I thank the Drawing Society, New York, and its President, Mr. James Biddle, for the commission of the book. Mr. Winslow Ames helped me patiently from start to finish, and far beyond the duties of an editor. Miss Felice Stampfle generously offered to revise the manuscript; she gave it the benefit of her linguistic acumen and of her experience as the editor of *Master Drawings*. Mrs. Agnes R. Claflin made valuable suggestions for improving the Introduction. I warmly thank Professor H. W. Janson who, as always, did not spare his counsel and help. I am grateful to my wife for encouragement and assistance. Sincere thanks are due to the publisher, especially to Mrs. Joanne Greenspun and Mr. Paul Anbinder. As always, the resources of the Frick Art Reference Library were invaluable for research. My greatest debt is to the friend to whom the book is dedicated. Without our lifelong exchange of thoughts, it never would have been written.

C. O. B.

Vassar College

November, 1969   Poughkeepsie, N.Y.

INTRODUCTION

William Kent
(1685–1748)

A Design for Landscaping a Hillside
British Museum, London

When I began to assemble this anthology and looked through hundreds of landscape drawings, I had the impression that nature is the most obvious theme of art. History does not bear out this notion. What by hindsight appears obvious was, in fact, a late discovery. Landscape, as an art form, like any other subject matter, does not exist naturally. To come into existence, it needed more than the keen eye which had been man's gift since prehistoric ages; it had to be in the mind first. It arose from a specific historical disposition, that of the early Renaissance.* Even then, landscape did not come forth readily, as if it had waited around the corner. Its growth was slow.

* This was recognized in Italy already in the sixteenth century (E. H. Gombrich, "Renaissance Artistic Theory and the Development of Landscape Painting," *Gazette des Beaux-Arts,* 1953, pp. 335 ff.).

The navigators explored the globe more systematically than the artists took possession of the world before their eyes. Only at the beginning of the sixteenth century did landscape become a theme in its own right, and about 1550 a fully articulated and diversified realm.

Strangely enough, at present landscape tends again to withdraw from art. We still appreciate the interpretations which former times gave of nature—perhaps even more fully than ever—but our own grasp seems to have become hesitant or arbitrary. Our covenant with nature has changed since the end of the last century. It is no coincidence that modern science has a totally new concept of matter and space. The future will show whether the eclipse of landscape is permanent or a passing phase.

This book deals with the past, and specifically with drawings. What is the role of drawing in the history of landscape? The majority of old master drawings were not ends in themselves, but served an ulterior purpose. A view of the countryside may be the outline for a topographical engraving, a layout of terrain may be the project for a park (see illustration, p. 13), a sketch of a thunderstorm the record for a treatise on meteorology. Most commonly, a drawing is made as a design for a painting or print, that is, a more elaborate and marketable product. In landscape, the step from the preliminary work to the final product can be of special interest because it is assumed that drawings usually were done in front of the motif, that they are observed "live," while paintings and prints had to be executed in the studio.

The facts, however, are not so clear-cut. Drawings of landscape do not always register an actual experience; and relatively few are closely related to paintings or prints, far fewer than is true of figure studies or of sketches for compositions. In landscape, the connection between drawings and finished works is loose. Most of the examples in this book had no ulterior use; they are to be appreciated in their own right as self-sufficient works. This does not always mean that they are end products. There is no rule that defines the last stage. This depends upon the draftsman's intent. A brief sketch may have satisfied him as a valid souvenir (plate 83), while an elaborate page has been superseded by one still more polished (plate 97). The great range of purpose makes the study of drawings endlessly absorbing.

A well-rounded history of landscape would have to be supported by both paintings and drawings. Drawings have merits which paintings lack. The open texture of lines and washes allows us to read them in the making. We accompany the artist "on the road"—not so much factually (because views were not always taken on the spot) as spiritually. We sense the formative process, with its mixture of observation and imagination. Paintings have their own virtues. The twentieth-century attitude leans so heavily on the improvised and spontaneous that we tend to forget that often only the fully elaborated work brings the artist's conception into its ultimate expressiveness and balance.

Neither paintings nor drawings alone can fully document the development of landscape sufficiently. From the early period, before 1500, drawings of landscape are virtually non-existent. Not many drawings have come down to us from the fifteenth century anyway, but the discrepancy in the number of surviving landscapes against those of other subjects makes it obvious that to *draw* landscape was not customary then, notwithstanding the vital role which it played in painting, both in the South and the North.

Through the centuries, the relative functions of painting and drawing vary. Roughly speaking, drawing leads the way in the sixteenth century when landscape begins to be a subject in its own right; it ranks as an equal in the seventeenth; and it carries on in the eighteenth century, when in painting the theme of landscape was obscured by genre and history. In the new trend of the early nineteenth century, drawing has a notable mission, but from then on, begins to recede. Painting became an outdoor occupation, color took on a new significance, and drawing lost some of its importance. Painting, especially in the loose strokes and dots of Impressionism, took over the exploratory role which had been the prerogative of drawing. These, however, are broad statements. In each country, almost with each artist, the function of drawing, the relation of drawing to painting, is different— the notes to the illustrations attempt to show this.

While this book does not tell the full story of landscape, it gives an idea of the great variety of ways in which European art interpreted this one theme, from Paradise to kitchen-garden. At a first glance, there seems to be little consistency in the manifold expressions. Landscape changes continuously and basically; every few pages, the reader has to adapt himself to the standard of another nation, of another era. Yet, after he has thumbed through the illustrations, he will be left with the impression that he has seen more than a motley assemblage and will sense a common aim. It is the attitude of the Western mind, the quest for a validity, in or beneath visible things, for something which binds them into a coherent and meaningful whole. This quest goes like a *leitmotiv* through the history of landscape and gives direction to the varying solutions.

I propose in the following pages to discuss some of those differences, as well as the constant *leitmotiv*. No complete survey is intended. I will try to steer clear of generalizations and to proceed pragmatically. My experience with individual drawings by a few masters will be presented.

A number of landscape drawings from the Italian *Quattrocento* still exist, and a sheet by Botticelli will be a suitable start (plate 2). It illustrates a scene from the *Divine Comedy,* the ascension of Beatrice and Dante from the earthly into the celestial Paradise. One cannot and should not dissociate the figures from the landscape; it is their unison which makes the story. The little grove provides the place of action: the middle region, the airy in-between

above the ground which the travelers have left, and below the sphere of the moon to which they are drawn. Yet also in a more relevant sense, the landscape partakes of the story by its overall liveliness and motion. The ground spreads, the trunks rise and bend, the branches arch and intersect, and expand into foliage. Even the circle above, drawn with a pair of compasses, is not simply round, but rounds itself. A common rhythm runs through the whole sheet and blends nature and figures. The landscape, while not described in detail, is animated and coherent.

Fra Bartolommeo's drawing (plate 8) does not relate an event, but we follow the spread and rise of the ground, the spacing of trees and buildings, the peasants, roads, and travelers with the same attention that we give to the progress of a narrative. Each part cooperates with the others, the trees are in place, they have the right volume and height, the hills are set at the right distance. Again, the whole is more than the sum of the parts.

Fra Bartolommeo's temperament differs from Botticelli's. His pen has another rhythm; his landscape does not have that almost metallic determination; it moves gently, at a leisurely pace. He is younger by one generation. The animation is broader and has more body and breath. His country has come down to earth, the aura is distinctly local. In fact, this might well be an actual Tuscan site near Florence. The validity of the landscape, however, does not lie in topographical accuracy. More is suggested than meets the eye: the country seems to extend beyond the borders of the sheet; and in telling of itself, it also conveys the clarity and richness of the land under the sky; the air is spiritual as well as atmospheric. And man has now been installed on earth. The human element is present, not only factually, i.e., in the houses and small figures; the entire landscape is tinged with it, and has become thoroughly habitable. The drawing is on the threshold of the six-teenth century.

The terms "activity" and "animation" try to capture a quality which, I believe, is basic in the art of that time. The two landscapes are not static but have a built-in potency, a quasi-autonomous life of their own, and not only in organic things like trees. An intrinsic animation pervades the country and makes it a coherent organism. When we read the drawings with a sort of empathy, participating in their activities, we get the "feel" of this aliveness; we also hear the overtones, understand their range and scope.

Perhaps the work of a great master of landscape can clarify this more convincingly (plate 6). Leonardo da Vinci's inert stones are as "active" as Botticelli's and Fra Bartolommeo's trees. The rocks are understood as weigh-ing down, rising upward, pressing against each other. But here, their activities have more significant connotations. The mountain not only shows how it actually functions, it also suggests its own potential, what it is able to do, and what can happen to it. Weights can shift, rocks can split, formations change. Parts under ground have come, or will come, to the surface, while others may crumble away under the erosion of weather. This and more is implied, and makes everything absorbing: the relative volumes and gravi-ties, the rounded and jagged shapes, the stable or precarious positions, the diagonal against the vertical directions, the lighted, shaded, or hidden sides. In grasping the potential with the visible, we understand the mountain in a wider extent and context. We see it as a part of the wide earth, and we comprehend nature's working.

To get the measure of Leonardo, the student will do well to glance through the corpus of his drawings before he concentrates on the land-scapes. He will be impressed not only by the diversity, but also by the persistent probing into certain themes. At the same time, he will notice that the single drawing is more eloquent when understood as part of a coherent research. Leonardo's avid curiosity is motivated by the insight that all things have a common constitution; this insight precedes the definition of specific facts. His discoveries, his constructions, his fictions explore exist-ence and its meaning as a whole. There is an affinity between a map and an anatomical design; currents of water have the same flow as blades of grass or strands of hair; the fingers of Mona Lisa are shaped by the same principle as the landscape at her back.

It has become customary to recognize a scientist's mind at work here. I believe that such an explanation limits rather than clarifies Leonardo's significance. True enough, the drawing of the rocks, as well as the grandiose *Alpine Valley with a Thunderstorm* (plate 5) served to illustrate geological or meteorological phenomena. The balled clouds, suspended between the steep mountains, the rain and shadow falling on the valley, the sunny heights above: these demonstrate the event graphically, the working of atmospheric pressure, the storm's range and limit. Yet the imagination reaches further: this site is a section of the multiform earth, this event one of many possible different ones which can happen on it. One thinks of other mountain ranges, plains, and towns; of becalmed weather, and earthshaking cataclysms. The relation to other forces is intimated so that one may compare the energy in the clouds with the different energy of a galloping horse. Yet all that is not stated as a theory but presented as an image; it is told in the peculiar language of art, with its unison of appearance and meaning. It is both outspoken and secretive, addressed not to the beholder's knowledge, but to his intuition. The landscapes of Leonardo go beyond the intent of science, certainly of science as it has become today.

With these remarks, I am trying to bring the *leitmotiv* into focus: a landscape is more than what it factually shows. Its overtones ask to be heard because they convey its scope, and they constitute the inner coherence. A landscape springs from a comprehensive vision, the total takes precedence over the parts. To scan such early works for details, with a magnifying glass, so to say, is scarcely the adequate approach. No doubt it can be pleasant to discover realistic observations, but these are subordinated to the unity and the true reality of the work. I always had difficulty in appreciating the famous drawing which Leonardo did at the age of twenty-one (plate 4). I knew that it was a key document, an historical first, but I could not "see" its significance until one day it dawned upon me that it should not be viewed too closely, but as from a distance, and not head on, but as from above. At once, it became a broad country under the sky, stretching in brilliant light, with a rich, yet coherent, morphology. More important, it took on a note of immediacy, of surprise, of coming-into-appearance, which I had not perceived as long as I was intent on its detail.

Overtones vary from artist to artist, and they are drastically different in the art of another nation. A landscape by the young Dürer seems to defy a comprehensive approach (plate 16). One suspects the drawing was done in stages, that Dürer was mainly interested in the structure of the rocks at the left, later adding the imaginary castle, the skyline, the gate, and the excited man at the bottom. And yet, what a synergistic force; one would not like to miss anything, one accepts the arbitrary combination because every part belongs. The impact of surprise and wonder stems not so much from the subject as from the way in which the entire landscape springs into presence, like a sudden apparition.

What overtones are there in Dürer's mountain? At first, it seems to lack a wider meaning altogether. Dürer stays with the objects, he clings to the stones, showing how they are: angular, curved; smooth, rough; vertical, horizontal; bare, or clothed with plants. But again, these are not mere statements of fact. The rocks are not taken for granted; Dürer creates or rather he recreates them, their labor to gain shape can be sensed. When our eye follows the pen lines (observe the contour of the horizon), we see that he does more than describe.

The German meets things at a level which the Italian disregards; it is their corporeality that absorbs him. He limns the stones meticulously and brings forth their irregular shapes and surfaces. Wölfflin remarked that "it is characteristic of German art that it has an acute understanding for materials, that it knows how matter feels about itself . . ."* Indeed, the beholder is on more familiar terms with Dürer's rocks and plants than with Leonardo's. Yet, from the ground floor of their material existence, Dürer makes things rise to eminence. They have to strive to clarify themselves, to reveal their essential meaning. As Dürer's art progresses, things become more and more articulate. It is instructive to compare the stones of this mountain with those in another drawing done several years later (plate 18). Now they lie more

* H. Wölfflin, *Die Kunst Albrecht Dürers,* 3rd ed., Munich, 1919, p. 138. "Es gehört zu den Eigentümlichkeiten der germanischen Kunst, dass sie ein starkes Stoffgefühl hat, dass sie weiss, wie es der Materie zumute ist . . ."

surely, their weights bear down more, they join in a genuine companionship. One may also compare the darkness in the crevices of the mountain with that in the forest, and then realize that in the latter it deepens more intensely. By the same token, the water is not simply dark, but darkens into the glossy blackness which the master likes to give to that element. Things now tell eloquently what they truly are, what the interior of a dense forest is, what a wellspring in the ground is. *A spring: this one, any one.*

The *View of Heroldsberg* (plate 19), from a time when Dürer had reached the fullness of his art, also lets "matter" express itself: the earth, the water of the pond, the sundry vegetation. The buildings emphasize their materials: the thatch of the roofs, the timber of the houses, the stone of the church. Here it is even more evident that physical properties are translated to a higher significance and that they are compounded into a whole. The village asks to be seen not frontwise, but from the ground upward, almost like a sculptural form; so that, rising within the hills, its colorful diversity clusters together with a singular energy. In German art, such unity is more poignant than in Italian art, because it seems to have been brought about with a greater effort.

In the early *Rocks with a Castle,* Dürer struggles to "extract art from nature" —his own words. *The Port of Antwerp* (plate 20) shows him in his sovereign maturity. The shapes are set down in their main features, almost without shading. Sea, landing place, boats, buildings have merged into one single conformation. The whole landscape has become the "thing." A comprehensive view is no longer difficult, it is demanded outright. Seen from above, the horizontal stretch of the water and the ground, and the varying heights of masts and towers are eloquent, the emptiness above them becomes dramatic,

and the space beyond the objects is as much "visible" as that in front of them.

What a mountain was to Dürer in his last years is demonstrated by a drawing of about 1527 (plate 21). The landscape has shed all local character; in fact, it is freely invented to illustrate a book on fortifications. The rock reaches to its height with a single thrust, and one senses that it also reaches far underground. In its compactness and volume, it has a grandeur that is reminiscent of the *Four Apostles* painting.

In Dürer's graphic *oeuvre,* landscapes are outnumbered by other subjects. As with Leonardo, it is worthwhile to leaf through a publication with many drawings, to study their inventiveness and diversity. Here, too, a totality comes forcibly to the mind. In drawing grasses in a meadow, a hare, the feathers of a bird's wing, a skull—each thing with its peculiar formation and surface—Dürer makes us aware of a common principle. His visual intelligence perceives a validity in the special case. The blue color of a feather tells about blueness, an oblique wooden peg about positions and materials in a wider sense. It was logical for Dürer to search for a module in his writings on art. What he explored there in theory, intuitively he had always known.

In the Netherlands, landscape flourished more than in any other country. Something in the temper of the Flemings and Dutch—perhaps a certain aloofness—drew them to an impersonal theme and let them find possibilities there which other nations saw in other fields.* From its beginning, Flemish

* See n. 1, above.

landscape was copious and articulate, as is known to the student who has looked at the countryside in the paintings of the Master of Flémalle or Jan van Eyck. However, no drawings of landscape are extant from fifteenth-century Flanders, nor from the early sixteenth, when Patinir introduced large vistas into religious paintings. A sheet by a follower of Patinir (plate 31) gives an idea of this artist's "world landscapes." A variegated country, literally seen from above, unrolls toward the high skyline.

In the hands of the great Pieter Bruegel, "world landscape" gains zest and a new meaning (plate 33). The penmanship is striking in its luxuriant texture, the drawing spins out a captivating yarn. Every square inch is filled: a lavish country, teeming with cattle, trees, houses, churches, towers, and walls, stretches upward to the distant mountains and clouds; an intense light shimmers on the surface. Bruegel's language is voluble, it expands one theme in endless variations. Paintings like the *Proverbs* or *Children's Games* aim at an encyclopedic completeness. This is the learned and didactic age of Rabelais and Montaigne.

The *Mountain Landscape with a River Valley,* a few years later, is less fantastic (plate 34). The very large sheet probably represents the Upper Rhine in the Alps, along which Bruegel wandered on his return from Italy. As with the preceding piece, the beholder cannot take in the country at one glance. He has to travel at walking speed, and take stock slowly. The journey is rewarding. In a sense, it is the landscape itself that travels. It moves along and spreads, venturous as an explorer who adds to his discoveries at each step. Every bit is novel: tree and stone, the irregular border of the river, the varying distances from boulder to boulder, and, most of all, the gradual climb of the towering mountain. Once this is recognized, the drawing is no longer an accumulation of objects, but a continuous and diversified country. Wandering in it becomes absorbing; it means moving through endless surprises, and also beyond the rectangle of the page. The imagination goes farther and farther into the infinite and unknown expanse of the earth.

Nevertheless, the beholder does not feel that he moves in a labyrinth. He is not lost; on the contrary, the orientation is rather easy. He follows the tale willingly. The threads meander and intersect, but they lie open and trace a plot. They provide bearings which were unknown before. Bruegel's world is articulated into domains: nature and mankind. Each has its standard and its rhythm.

In the Rhine valley, the overall measure is set by the mountain, eminent in grandeur. The steps downward, to the moderate elevation of the castle-hill, further down to the bottomland, are gauged by that standard. Each region has its feature and stature. Trees and boulders too have their specific heights and volumes, and their appointed places in the organism.

The rhythm of nature is very slow. The river carries on with a leisure that knows no beginning nor end. The land hardly seems to take notice of the changing seasons and the cycles of the years. Hence the steadiness and assurance which make the country so imposing.

Compared with the standard of nature, the human domain seems to be pathetically slight. Man moves within a narrow space, he has only scratched the surface of the earth. His settlements are toylike, and his pursuits short-lived. The hamlet has grown as if by itself, not by planning. The compound of the castle has expanded in a haphazard manner, with new parts added one at a time, as they were needed.

At second thought, one corrects this impression. The people too have their place on earth, and the right to use it—working, traveling, or loafing. Their doings are small, but legitimate and persistent. Man leaves a stamp which is more incisive than his physical radius and weight would warrant. Bruegel is considerate to him, he even wishes us to look at nature from *his* point of view. We ask how far the river is navigable, we look for an easy road across the mountains, and estimate the length by walking time. The country appears "empty" for the very reason that few people are in it.

Bruegel has turned a new leaf in the history of landscape. From now on, nature will be unthinkable without man and his life. To Bruegel, people too are "nature"—thoroughly intermixed with nature in the usual meaning. He often plays upon the two aspects of the term. In his *Tower of Babel* (Vienna), the humans vainly try to outbuild the limits of their station. Of necessity, their product returns to the domain of nature. The top of the tower is surrounded by clouds, the colossal pile ignores the antlike bustle; it begins to decay, and the tenants return to their own level, make their "natural" abode in it, hang out the laundry and put flowerpots on the windowsills.

From the same time as that painting, 1563, may also date the *Marine Landscape, with a View of Antwerp* (plate 36). It is of Bruegel's dramatic period, from which no other landscape drawings exist. The water fills nearly the entire surface; Bruegel gives a graphic account of the waves, of their diverse shapes and lively crisscrossing. Together they have an intense force and build up the plot of the story: the sea as a whole, one body, set against storm and light; the human element at the fringes, or dispersed within. That the action is staged in sight of Antwerp, at the artist's doorstep, provides an added poignancy. But the story would be almost equally effective in a nameless locality because it carries its own message of the precariousness of human endeavor. Understandably, scholarly research has looked for precise allegorical connotations, yet the lesson is palpable enough without them. Bruegel does not preach, he rather lets us find the moral ourselves. He also knows that there are two sides to everything. There is ample elbowroom in his works, physically and morally.

It is somewhat reckless to draw general conclusions about the evolution of landscape from such few examples. Even so, I think, the direction is apparent. The sixteenth century has inherited the concept of an all-inclusive and coherent world. It maintains this concept, but subdivides the total. It becomes aware of differing categories which jointly support the whole. When we compare paintings of Perugino and Raphael, we find that Raphael has sundered earth from sky explicitly: the ground takes on weight, human bodies stand or sit on it more corporeally, the sky vaults. He also separates the worldly from the celestial realm and makes the two interact. A similar unfolding takes place from Bellini to Titian, from Gerard David to Patinir. Most important, of course, is the distinction between the domains of nature and man, as we observed in the art of Bruegel. Naturally, this did not happen abruptly. Van Eyck's carpet-like landscape was gradually transformed—Memling and Patinir are major stages—until Bruegel could weave the fabric of his tales.

The next century achieves a new synthesis. In doing so, it fulfills the aim of the preceding times and brings European landscape to its culmination—

if such can be said in history. In Holland, it is the golden age, the era which produced Rembrandt.

Landscape is not a large part of Rembrandt's *oeuvre:* about one-sixth of the drawings are devoted to it, even fewer prints and paintings. He turned to landscape rather late, towards 1640, when he already was a renowned painter of portraits and religious subjects. His first ventures into the new field, for example, *A Village Before a Thunderstorm* (plate 88), have the emphatic tone of his Biblical stories at that period. The village passes through a momentous event, the silent engagement between the cottages and the threatening storm. The house in front is the main actor. We are enjoined to side with it, to feel how it pits itself against the glaring sunshine and the dark clouds. The low building gains stature in undergoing and resisting the weather, and becomes a personality of sorts.

This first quasi-dramatic stage gives way to a different attitude (the gradual change can be studied in the etchings of the 1640s). In *The Bend in the Amstel River* (plate 89), the tension has disappeared. Now it is the entire landscape that speaks as a personality. Remembering Bruegel, one realizes what a change has taken place in the intervening hundred years. Instead of a finespun texture, the lines and washes are applied in broad strokes. The story is unified; a single glance puts us into the country. We are in the plain of Holland, and share its quiet sunny day. Not much happens: a pair of horsemen slowly moves along the road, some people seem to be busy in the boats, a man is seated on a bench at the right. A concentrated stillness reigns all around, to the far distance, under the vast sky. What has become of the "domains"? Evidently, they are merged into a comprehensive living space. And now, it is the country that dominates; people

and their doings are accommodated in it, but relegated to a secondary role.

The drawing speaks to the beholder intensely. He is invited more strongly than before to enter the landscape, to participate in its life—a life which is more integrated than in previous times, one which is the common pulsebeat of the whole. Can this be defined more clearly?

I should like to make a short digression to consider a drawing by a contemporary of Rembrandt, Jan van Goyen (plate 84). Here, too, is a rural neighborhood on a working day. In order to comprehend its life, the beholder will read it as *proceeding.* At once, the landscape begins to unfold and to tell its story. Peasants, wagon, windmill go their ways, and so do the birds, the clouds, the water. Everything shares in the goings-on, everything is about its business. The variant speed patterns can be distinguished: the moving wagon's from the faster birds', from the sitting and waiting angler's, and these from the slow and steady circuits of tide and day. They all are graduated in their respective gaits, yet synchronized and simultaneous; and together they constitute an overall motion. Above the polyphony of the sundry speeds, the procession of the whole can be sensed, almost heard, like the hum of a workshop. There is a common rhythm: a gradual coming and departing, in which the present moment is a slight crescendo. The pace is leisurely but persistent, and all goes on as it has to do. For the process is repetitious: tomorrow, too, the birds will fly, and so day after day, as they have always done; ebb and tide will alternate, the peasants attend to their work. The boats have been at their job many times, and know where they are bound. Each and every thing has its direction and reliability.

It is by going along with the landscape that the beholder finds the key to its rhythm and spirit. He reads it in time as well as in space; the two dimensions are but aspects of a single quality. And, needless to say, time is not appended to the objects as an addition. Their *proceeding* is their very breath and meaning. It is the groove which existence has found, where the "animation," the "activity," of earlier times has found its full articulation.

Van Goyen provides an easy access to the art of seventeenth-century Holland. His language is uncomplicated "basic Dutch" (M. J. Friedländer). Rembrandt is more demanding. His country asserts itself powerfully, and conveys a more substantial message.

To Rembrandt, the process does not go on here, there, and everywhere, as to Van Goyen, but on a broad front. It carries along as one comprehensive stream, that of the landscape as a whole. Moreover, its rhythm is different. Van Goyen's is a fleeting now, again, and always—even, relaxed, and contented. Rembrandt's does not drift. Time passes, but it lasts. What has gone by is not lost, but has accumulated, has become an integral part of the country, its own possession. And this gives to its "now" an emphasis which exceeds by far the crescendo of Van Goyen. The landscape lights up from the past into the present stage, it has reached a plateau, the height of its existence. A temporary height, though. For it will continue from here: the way points forward, with a note of assurance which should not be missed. The country moves on, yet keeps its identity. The beholder feels it passing and, at the same time, comprehends the sum of its existence.

This great vision also makes *The Nieuwe Meer* (plate 90) so enthralling. One senses the huge volume of the past from which the day has emerged, and the future into which it will merge. Against this background, the advance of the boat, the light wind over the water, the ripple in the rushes gain something unique and precious.

The country has plenty of time, and invites us to share in it. It appears so unconstrained that we may overlook an essential feature: the *must* in the proceeding, the necessity of all that happens. The steady motion of the vessel, the bending of the rushes—however fleeting and incidental they are—bespeak something inevitable and irrevocable. The country almost seems to be conscious of it, and to know that it is subject to its fate. The stillness is not merely one of peace, but of awe.

In those years about 1650, landscape must have meant much to Rembrandt. He took his walks around Amsterdam,* from which he brought home the drawings of the canals and dikes, the church of Diemen, the manor Kostverloren, and the many farmsteads under elm trees (plate 91). He went to these and other places many times, and drew the same localities repeatedly. Yet each drawing is a separate entity. The individuality of this farm does not rely upon anything factual, such as the form of the building or the location under these trees, alongside the water. It rather consists in the uniqueness of its "life," which it shares with no other place. The very air between the trees, the mirroring of the water, the hour of the day are no less individual than the tangible objects. Everything is a necessary and inseparable part in the identity of the farmstead, which exists only once, in its own space and time.

Going through the master's landscape drawings, one observes that people play a minor role. Either the land is empty, or the inhabitants are few and unobtrusive. A peasant goes about his way, enters a door, or leans out of a window. Occasionally, a seated draftsman (in whom one likes to see the artist) sketches a house. On the other hand, buildings *belong,* they are regular

* F. Lugt, *Mit Rembrandt in Amsterdam,* Berlin, 1920.

and conspicuous items, and bring to mind the people who live there. In fact, the human species is not omitted, but subordinated. Rembrandt seems to feel—consciously or not—that a livelier human presence would alter the tone. Probably for the same reason, birds in flight are rare, while swans and ducks in the water occur frequently. Rembrandt is always precise in the indication of the specific genre. When figures are prominent in a landscape, it strikes a note quite distinct from that of an empty landscape.

A drawing (plate 93) somewhat earlier than the preceding one shows a different kind of landscape, a vista of Venetian ancestry. The stress is on the group in front, on the Biblical hunter Nimrod, resting with his horse and hounds. The river valley with the bridge, the cleft mountains covered with fantastic castles, supply resonance to the story. Can we make the connection to the domestic landscapes? Yes, in a measure. Here, too, is the past accumulated, here is the climax of the present hour, the pervasive stillness which absorbs passing incidents. The repose of Nimrod is beautifully underlined by the protective height of the mountain. However, the imagination is channeled in a more specific direction, away from the native past into that of the Patriarchs, wandering with their herds in older countries. Here, Rembrandt parallels the landscape of history which flourished in Rome at the same time.

It is a curious fact that a signal contribution to the Italian *Seicento* was made by two outsiders, the Frenchmen Nicolas Poussin and Claude Lorrain. The two came from different provinces of France; their temperaments were far apart, but both gave to the South something that was outside the range of Italian thinking. Poussin's images belong to the great statements of the Gallic mind. Also Claude Lorrain, of whom the following pages treat, has to be understood as a Frenchman, not as "Roman," notwithstanding the fact that Rome and her countryside were his locale, that he gave to the so-called classical landscape its conclusive form.

It strikes us, coming from Netherlandish art, that the *View of Saint Peter's* (plate 60) is more polished and clear-cut. The skyline is meticulously limned, the cupola sharply contoured. Distances are exactly defined: one marks the interval between the towers of the wall, from Saint Peter's to the hills, from the ground to the flock of birds. The drawing speaks with a limpid clarity, at an exact pitch. The elevation of a hill, the height of the church, each has a specific timbre, of resonance and contrast: the small cupola is echoed by the immense vault of the sky, the hills stand raised in contrast to the hollow of the valley.

In a late drawing—the *Landscape with Mount Soracte* (plate 63)—the relations are even more precise: observe the intervals between the *single* birds, the space between foreground and mountain range. The altitude at which we find ourselves is so distinctly conveyed that we feel we are breathing mountain air.

Like Netherlandish landscapes, those of Claude carry intimations of a vaster country. But the overtones are not the same. In the North, the space that is beyond is contiguous to the landscape, its gradual extension. Claude sets the stakes farther out, and it is the wide earth as a whole that seems to encircle his landscapes. This is the great yardstick by which he measures;

and as soon as we are aware of it, everything falls into place. The extent of the Roman valley, the size of Saint Peter's, become relative to the wider country. The vast plateau of the *Landscape with the Baptism of the Eunuch* (plate 64) is encompassed by a vaster geography. The distances within also are gauged by the same measurements: the intervals between the trees, from trees to figures, are sections of an overall space. Even a tiny corner of nature, like that of the *Brook and Trees* (plate 62), evokes the beyond, becomes articulate by resonance and contrast. One feels the sheltering of this place, the assurance of the "here" and, at the same time, the open expanse all around and above.

Therefore, the imagination ranges with a singular freedom. Standing in a harbor, at the border of the sea, we do not travel progressively away, we think of other harbors, of different countries, of other latitudes far removed. The beauty and comfort of the place where we stand are enhanced by the allurement of foreign lands.

No wonder that Claude's works are full of travelers: Europa on the bull embarks upon her sea voyage, Hagar departs for the desert, the Queen of Sheba arrives at the palace of Solomon, the Holy Family rests on the flight to Egypt. The list could easily be enlarged because everybody in his world is itinerant, certainly the herds, the deer and, above all, the birds in the air. And there are the places and implements of voyage: the roads crossing the plains, the open sea, the bridges, lighthouses, ships of all shapes and sizes, anchors, ropes, and chests.

It will be remembered that Rembrandt, too, has a liking for the wayfaring kind. Claude's emphasis is different: not on the traveler himself, but on traveling; not the person, and what he portends, but the cause of travel-

ing. Such is the bent of the French mind: it thinks in impersonal, objective categories—a mentality which singles it out from the other nations.

Hence, life presents to Claude a particular facet. The presence and occupations of people do not seem to derive from their personal motives, but from habit and established custom, a custom to which Claude gives the dignity of a tradition. The way in which goatherds tend their flocks, or a woman is seated on the ground, has a measure of ceremony, of nobility. In the historical paintings, the observation of manners, of decorous habits is even more distinct. It speaks in the stateliness of a procession, in a meeting and leave-taking. Assisting servants, and sailors who load the baggage, do as their station and function demand.

Indeed, all of Claude's world is ennobled by a patina of tradition. The temples with columns, the palaces, the carved ships' hulls, their elaborate tackle tell of it; and no less the products of small crafts: carpets, dresses, musical instruments. All these man-made objects are the result of taste and skill, practical as well as ornate, tokens of a long-standing civilization.

History, as Claude understands it, does not confront us with the momentous situations of Poussin. Our honored past comes alive; a page from the Bible, from Homer, or Vergil is opened, their episodes are reenacted. We do not ask why and how they came about, and do not learn anything new from them. They rather endorse our cherished heritage. *The Baptism of the Eunuch* reads more like a legend than Acts 8: 26–39; Hagar's plight relates the story whose happy end we know (in fact, the desert is filled with a luscious growth). Even in the majestic *Sermon on the Mount* (The Frick Collection, New York), a contemplative and sociable ambience is more evident than the significance of the Beatitudes.

I have reported these cultural and historical features because they have been overlooked formerly. Only recently has art criticism become aware of their importance.* Of course, they have to be understood within the wider context of Claude's art. Beyond the human sphere is that of nature. Nature, too, has her tradition, and of a caliber larger than man's, not merely long-standing but eternal. "Eternal" would be out of place for Dutch landscape, where the duration is left indeterminate—hence the mysterious note in Rembrandt's landscapes. French thinking prefers finite quantities. To Claude, earth, sea, sky exist forever. Again, he states it in antithetic language: the short waves against the ageless ocean, the transitory sunset against the eternal firmament.

The histories of nature and of man do not have the same rhythm, but they interlock. It is rewarding to observe how nicely Claude connects and differentiates them. Trees, while in reality more short-lived than buildings, are lodged with a greater, a more "natural," sureness. Conversely, a building, while grounded in nature, accentuates the land and sets up a landmark. The stability and dignity of an old oak accords and contrasts with the wanderer who dwells in its shade. Such interrelations are manifold, the two realms are geared to each other solidly and delicately.

What they have in common is the "now." It lights up with a crystalline clarity that is Claude Lorrain's alone. His contemporaries must have felt it when they commended his skill in rendering the silvery light of morning or the glow of sundown. Yet, more than this is involved. The "light" is the ring of the hour, which brings the landscape, and all that exists and happens in it, into actuality. We read it most easily from an actual event, as in *The*

* M. Roethlisberger, *Claude Lorrain, The Paintings,* New Haven, 1961, Vol. I, p. 23.

Baptism of the Eunuch, where the figures are the visible focus of actuality, and the entire surroundings seem to look and to listen. But even when nothing happens, or figures are absent, there is the same note of suspense. In the "here and now," Claude gives us the essence of his art: the unique, spotless, exalted hour shining forth from a timeless background.

I have tried to show in some measure why the seventeenth is the *grand siècle* of landscape. Indeed that era found some of the most valid insights ever, and still is, I believe, a spiritual home to which our minds can turn for wisdom and comfort. Thereafter, history swings in another direction.

Skipping any gradual transition, we cross a century and move from Rome to Paris; also, it appears, into a more limited field (plate 105). Boucher leads us to a secluded corner of a park, where trees and trellises restrict the view. A boy is fishing from a small wooden bridge; a young woman looks back at the dog on the near side—a homely scene, soberly presented, and indifferent to the wide reaches of space and time, to the overtones which reverberate in the landscape of previous times.

Of course, Boucher is not to be measured with the standards of a period to which he does not belong. The very pleasure which he affords indicates that his matter-of-factness is of a special kind. To be sure, the drawing talks prose, not poetry, but the prose of the *dixhuitième,* which knows how to formulate. It is a common experience that a neatly worded statement makes the listener smile—this happens in front of such a work. It goes straight to the point, like a well-turned sentence of Voltaire. One observes

RENNER LEARNING RESOURCES CENTER
ELGIN COMMUNITY COLLEGE
ELGIN, ILLINOIS

the position and structure of the bridge, the places and sizes of the trees, the alternation of shadow and light, the postures of the figures, and the correlation of all this—not the slightest vagueness remains, everything is lucid and convincing.

Things and persons are not merely described, they are *defined,* and they gratify the intellect no less than the eye. Boucher characterizes them, he shows of what sort they are, and also unfolds their different layers of meaning. The bridge, for example, in the first place, is a square and simple construction of timber, built close above the water. Then, it is the passageway for crossing the brook; and third, a rustic, makeshift fixture which contrasts with the stateliness of the park. Similarly, we appraise the other parts: the ill-kept fence, the beautiful trees. We think of maintenance and utility, of seclusion and leisure. We also ask what sort of people these youngsters are, what their business is here; we gauge their station by dress and behavior.

In other words, Boucher places everything in its proper category. He conveys the typical within the specific. Clearly, here is an order of a new kind, that of the Age of Reason. Boucher is its perfect representative, though not its greatest; he is the logician of the Rococo. His suites of the Four Seasons, of the Crafts and Occupations, of Deities, mark generic concepts; each painting means exactly what the label says. In art, however, logic has to be taken with a grain of salt. Boucher does not expound theories, but imparts his notions directly; he blends rational and visual intelligence. A blue is the color of the sky, and, at the same time, it bespeaks the celestial realm, Heaven with a capital *H.*

It stands to reason that such an approach stresses the diversity of objects rather than their unison. Yet their coherence is obvious in this drawing:

an interplay of opposites, a witty combination, an accidental facet of contemporary life. A work of Boucher brings forth a situation, each a different one, out of many possibilities. To be sure, his vocabulary is relatively limited; but he shuffles his deck again and again, and produces a new combination.

Boucher looks tame when compared to his great pupil (plate 106). Fragonard spreads a garland of trees and vines in one spirited gesture, with a buoyancy that seems to defy orderly distinctions and to be free of any restraint. The drawing is an early work done in Naples. The color of the sanguine lends it a particular sparkle.

To comprehend the scope of Fragonard, one should look not only at his landscapes, but also at genre, portraits, and animals. The aggressive youth, the bashful or the naughty girl, the bulky Oriental, the alert dog, the obtuse bull: their conformation, posture, action and reaction are caught. Fragonard characterizes them, as Boucher does, but he goes deeper, to the core of their vitality, grasping its force and nuance. He understands the mixture of reason and instinct in human beings, feels their impulses, restrained (though not always) by education and decorum. Their "animal spirits" draw them into the hazards of life; they are less calculable than Boucher's, there is no telling what they may do, what will happen to them.

To Fragonard, everything is fraught with adventure. Not without reason is he fond of swings, ladders, and scaffolds. The umbrella pines in the Roman park (plate 107) tower high above the statues and the tiny figures, the light contrasts dynamically with the shade; the stairs, without railing, are dangerously steep. Also in these well-tended surroundings, he reaches for the elemental; they are free from the taint of provincialism in Boucher's park.

There is also a singular quickness in his grasp: the peaceful scene seems to emerge suddenly, as out of nowhere, evoked for just this moment, and without thought of before and after. The drawing, done with the brush, in transparent inks, dates from his second journey to Italy, in 1773/74.

Fragonard himself is not carried away by all this vehemence. He is French, which means that he is objective, critical. He never lets things get out of his control. The trees rise exactly to the height that is wanted, the intensity of sunshine is determined. In a love story, the girl may be flustered beyond restraint, but her rapture is viewed with detachment. Fragonard coins the irrational in nature and humans into a rational image. In fact, what delights us most in his art is the uncanny sureness and the flexibility with which he handles the diverse subjects and complicated situations.

The eighteenth century speaks a pointed language; its formulation is concise, the rhythm short. Usually, landscape shuns the vast spaces,* it prefers the middle distance, is fond of gardens, staffed with present-day people. This is a sophisticated age, the last stage of a long development. From mid-century on, art is groping towards new issues. The final break comes about 1800.

In a museum, when going from the old masters to the nineteenth century, one enters another climate. The modern visitor, used to crossing spiritual

frontiers, adjusts himself automatically to the change, perhaps all too easily. He is hardly conscious of being in new surroundings, where the very air is different and where the old bearings have been supplanted by new ones.

Two drawings, one by Claude Lorrain (plate 63), the other by Corot (plate 125), present the same locality, the Tiber Valley near Civita Castellana, with Mount Soracte in the background. But how far apart are they in spirit!

The first reaction to Corot is that this is a *real* place. The skyline of the mountain, the old monastery, our distance to them, all this strikes us as authentic. We do not doubt that the landscape looks as Corot depicted it with the crisp lines of his pen. However, we have become wary of the slippery term "reality"; we know that a photograph would be even more faithful, but also, that it would lack something which only the artifact contains. Here, too, is more than a mechanical transcript: there is a context from which the view derives its true reality.

First, there is the context of knowledge. Corot's Soracte has its place on the map. It is a landmark in the topography of Italy, the isolated ridge which the traveler recognizes when nearing Rome from the north. It is also a landmark in poetry. Vergil and Horace have celebrated it, and, in Corot's time, Byron in *Childe Harold*. Connotations of geography and history have somehow found their way into Corot's work.

Moreover, an overtone of emotion swings about it. One senses the affection of the northerner for the land where nature and civilization fuse so harmoniously, for the venerable country which is part of his own culture. This image was in young Corot's mind even before he set foot on Italian soil, and now he happily captures it "live." During the summer of 1826,

---

* J.-J. Rousseau observed: "The predilection for vistas has its root in the tendency of most men to feel at home only where they are not at the moment" (Eva Maria Neumeyer, "The Landscape Garden as a Symbol in Rousseau, Goethe and Flaubert," *Journal of the History of Ideas,* 8, 1947, p. 194).

he explores the Campagna and the mountains, he draws an old town, a castle on the hilltop, a cluster of trees, a rocky riverbed, all in the southern light—"lumière désespérante pour moi," he writes. Each is a "crystalline vision" (Kenneth Clark), a page in his compendium of the Eternal City and its environs.

"This is the place," says the drawing, a locality whose name one wishes to know. How little does the name "Soracte" count in the country of Claude! There, the identity springs from other sources and has another meaning. Corot's Soracte is pointedly singular, and at the same time anchored in a solid frame of reference, *one* case within the Italy of his notions and affection.

Corot's first stay in Rome marked the beginning of a lifelong succession of travels, mostly to a province in France, but also to Switzerland, Holland, London, and again to Italy. He became one of the many itinerant artists of the century, perhaps the most assiduous one. It is the regional character of the places that attracts him. He captures the specific light and color— the radiant blue of the Mediterranean at Genoa, the hazy blue of the Ile-de-France and the again different hue of the Lake of Geneva. He describes the shape of the terrain—"le beau terrain"—and has a keen eye for its stone. "One meets in a painting a stack of piled boulders, in another a bare rock, ready to be cut, and one is surprised how sensitively the artist reveals the essence of this beautiful material."* He observes the style of architecture, which together with the land constitutes the distinct character of a landscape.

What is novel in his approach will be more evident when we realize that

* Translated from F. Rintelen, *Reden und Aufsätze,* Basel, 1927, p. 67.

our position as beholders also has changed. We have become outsiders, we stand in front of the landscape. We follow the recession towards Mount Soracte, and measure the exquisite distances; we also can proceed in the opposite direction and feel the country stretching towards us. There is a *vis-à-vis* of here and there, and not only in space; it is rather a discourse between subject and object.

Who are *we* now? To begin, "we" is not quite correct. The country is meant for the single person. One is alone with it, and surveys it with the pleasant sensation of isolation and calm that befits the solitary traveler—with the attitude of a tourist, as it were, of an intelligent and sensitive tourist who is enriched by a visit to Civita Castellana. Yet there is more to it, as will be apparent from a landscape of Corot's mature years (plate 126). The valley near Morestel is filled with an intense poetic mood which engages not only the affectionate interest of the beholder, but his whole being. For here is not merely a lovely spot in France, typical of one of her provinces. The landscape conveys the beauty of all nature; it is part of the earth, the hospitable earth, where man has his physical and spiritual home. It seems to invite the beholder intimately, to give him a pledge of comfort and peace. This message is repeated again and again, by the route to Marissel, the valley of Ville-d'Avray, or a road with a farmhouse—unpretentious, but places where the meadows and the air, where every tree and leaf bespeak the concord of nature and man.

The landscape addresses the beholder in a guarded language, though. He is not supposed to trespass into it and to stroll around. He remains on his side. Some paintings veto an intrusion visually by laying a curtain of trees over the picture plane.

Allusions to change and motion are rare in the work of Corot. One does not expect that the day will fade. People usually do not move around; they stand or sit. The traffic in the *Harbor of La Rochelle* (Yale Art Gallery, New Haven) is virtually at a standstill; a few laborers are busy in what appears to be a commercial backwater. As Corot grows older he is more and more averse to change, and relies on the quietness and stability of existence. Even an anti-modern attitude can be sensed. To my knowledge, Corot never represented machines; still, he used the railway on his travels. All that is rooted in the past is venerable to him; so the bridge of Mantes which spans the river for ages. The motionless water of a pond, which often recurs in his late works, is an almost symbolic expression of his feeling for permanence.

The era around 1800 made the most radical break in the concept of landscape since the *Quattrocento*. It introduced a different reality. Landscape becomes the mirror of insights and beliefs, of the artist's *Weltanschauung*.* From now on, art will be personal art. The intellectual and moral explorations will be daring, contradictory, and sometimes bewildering.

The bond between nature and man, which Corot affirms endearingly, is problematic to others. Courbet and the Barbizon painters (plates 132, 133) stress their incongruity. An oversized tree, an isolated shepherd in an endless plain, a sinister sky contrast the immensity of nature and the littleness of man. But all this is viewed from *our* angle. The expanse is wide because we feel lonely in it, the tree enormous because it exceeds our life-span and we have to lift our eyes up to it. The earth is low, for the peasant has to bend down, and the soil is heavy for him. The standard is set by man, even when nature is indifferent or hostile.

The landscape of the Impressionists tells further of the human condition, but in a less dogmatic tone. It hints rather than spells out. The suggestions of contemporary life, of social modes are made to appear casual, and often are so discreetly touched upon that some of them may escape the beholder. I wonder whether in Manet's painting of an empty garden we can discern all the allusions—summer, vacation, Sunday afternoon, suburb, visitors, leisure, boredom, and more.** The same is true for Degas, Pissarro, Renoir, Monet. Behind the varied themes and the colorful surfaces is a denominator, a concept of life, for each artist a different one. The term "impressionism" is misleading, because it obscures the intellectual acumen, the probing into every conceivable direction—the attitude of a scientific, experimenting age.

About 1870, landscape has become oversensitized, and so charged with subtle connotations that it seems inconceivable that it can go further in the same direction. Suddenly though, history has one of her surprises. A new door opens: the art of Cézanne.

Cézanne, too, is a researcher, as his persistent investigations of the Mont Sainte Victoire prove (plate 142). What dissociates his mountain from Corot's Soracte? Why do we know that a comparison would be ludicrous? The two mountains rise into different air, physically and spiritually. The former references, the connotations of locality and civilization—all that has been abandoned, and something independent stands there. Cézanne's mountain is an autonomous being. It does not even belong to the domain of nature

---

* A writer of that time, H.-F. Amiel (Geneva, 1821–1881) went so far as to say "Un paysage est un état d'âme" (a landscape is a state of the soul).

** How will it appear to the student of the year 2100? An iconographical commentary will not help him; the message is all implied.

in the accepted sense; the matter of which it consists is disregarded. The significance seems to lie in the mere form. Is this an abstraction then, the reduction to stereometric figures, to "cylinder, sphere, and cone"—to repeat the artist's own words, quoted so often?*

An artist is not necessarily his own most competent interpreter. When Cézanne's remark is checked against his art, it needs to be qualified. In practice, his procedure is anything but mathematical. The lines approach and encompass the objects rather than delimit them, the contours consist of several strokes of varying strength, in a broken succession (plate 141). They complicate as well as clarify the form—the opposite of a design on a geometrical drafting board. And, taking the layout as a whole, we find that one object cannot be understood without the others, that together they enact a configuration of similarity and diversity. Furthermore, they comprise the space which is around them: the space in front, between, and behind the *massif* of Sainte Victoire is an integral part of it, no longer the meeting area between landscape and beholder.

To get the bearings of this art, one cannot interpret it as an "abstraction," that is, in a negative sense. Here, too, is a positive credo, and Cézanne strove during all his life to bring it to its *réalisation*. Renoir told the critic Geffroy: "It was an unforgettable sight to watch Cézanne at his easel; painting, looking at the landscape; he was truly alone in the world, ardent, attentive, respectful."** Indeed, a work of Cézanne is charged with intensity; all things have to give their best to achieve what he demands from them. They labor

to come into their own, every stroke and every nuance of shade count. The trunks and branches of trees, in their relative thickness, straight or curving, in oblique and upright stances, crossing or not crossing: they struggle towards the maximum of visual intelligibility, and the outcome is this very configuration, just so and no different. The mountain has to show the height of its twin tops, the rise and descent of the shoulders, at just these angles, with every inflection of the contours, the progressive protruding towards the bottom, and the footing within the base of smaller hills. Each thing has its task, and together they constitute a "thing" of a more complex order: that constellation of contrast and harmony which a landscape of Cézanne is. It took an unending effort to shape the figure of Sainte Victoire, dominating, simple, and complex. The master's steady and obstinate progress to his mature style is fascinating—not unlike Rembrandt's.

Does Cézanne then present only the visual aspect of nature devoid of any deeper significance? Why do we know that he imparts something important to us? For the first time in history, landscape speaks on its own terms, without admixture of other elements and without relying on a spiritual background. The Mont Sainte Victoire, in being itself, only itself, of *this* conformation, tells what a mountain, what mountainness is: rise, massiveness, spaciousness. The successive chains of rolling country near Gardanne (plate 140), accented with buildings, bounded by the utterly delicate skyline, under the mass of sky, are a statement about reclining and spreading. Cézanne's landscapes teach fundamental facts, they show what height and depth are, what proximity and distance, light and dark are, how land contrasts with a body of sea, how plains display their shades and colors. All this, and more, in an endless variation, is what he understood by "nature." The word

*   In a letter to Emile Bernard of 1904, which one should read with a grain of salt. Bernard was always looking for handy theories. Cézanne remarked that he had a "tempérament de raisonneur," that he was an "intellectuel, congestionné par les souvenirs des musées" (letters to his son, 22nd and 26th September 1906).

**   Translated from Geffroy, *La Vie Artistique,* III, Paris, 1894, p. 256.

comes up again and again in letters and conversations. His is not the nature of geology, of vegetative growth, of weather; yet it *is* nature, understood as a totality and in basic principles. Therefore, it means so much to us; it shows us our *nourritures terrestres.* If, in afterlife, we were granted a token of remembrance from this earth, perhaps it would be one of Cézanne's pine trees or emerald fields which we would cherish most.

Cézanne knew that he was ahead of his time. In 1896, he wrote to Gasquet: "Perhaps I have come too early. I was the painter of your generation rather than of mine."* He started the quest of the twentieth century. His own place, however, is with the nineteenth. He was convinced that his art was nature clarified and organized, that reality could be mastered. A problematic task at that stage—how much so is evident in the struggle of Van Gogh.

He was fourteen years younger than Cézanne, but the *Suburb of Paris* (plate 145) is, in a sense, more traditional than the older master's Gardanne. The connotations which Cézanne had dropped remain important to Van Gogh. Here is the *banlieue,* where houses and factories are crowding out the open fields; an industrial section of the modern city, active and messy. Van Gogh is attentive to the purpose of a street, to the weather. He thinks of the people who have to live and work there; he feels the dreariness of their existence. Compared to his smokestacks, those of Pissarro or Monet look carefree.

Van Gogh owed much to France, but he belongs to it only in part. In his heart, he is Dutch. It is the synthesis of Dutchness with the art of his adopted country that released his full genius and made him the eminent master at a turning point in history.

What is Netherlandish here? Perhaps it is an empathy with things, an understanding for their behavior. Van Gogh describes them in great detail. He specifies the stones and the ground, he registers the single stakes of the fence and the windows in the houses, he follows the road and the recession of the terrain. The total is imposing; it brings to mind Pieter Bruegel's world landscapes. But as soon as the two are mentioned together—as has been done often—the gulf that separates them becomes evident. Van Gogh cannot, and does not wish to, come to terms with the world in the same way that Bruegel did three hundred years earlier. He has to question it and to build it anew. He places the trees, assembles the fences, and sets the bend of the street. Nothing is taken for granted, not even the horizontality of the earth. Van Gogh seems to lift it off its hinges, and reset it into place. That he does so through an inner necessity can be felt in the mounting intensity of the three drawings reproduced here.

The *Fields and Farmhouses near Arles* (plate 146), like the Parisian *banlieue,* evokes the life of the people; but, here, in harmony with nature. The sun means not only light, but also heat and crops; the houses tell of coolness and shelter, and the spread of the field denotes the ambit of the farmer's work.

Again, Van Gogh builds the surface from particles. With changing strokes and dots, with different inks, he produces an irregular texture of a wonderful freedom and strength, suggestive of more than vegetative life. He himself compared the plains of Provence to the surface of the sea,** but one may disregard a concrete meaning altogether. In fact, the patterns of the wallpapers which the artist invented in the backgrounds of portraits are no less expressive. Something essential seems to become visible.

* J. Rewald, *Paul Cézanne, Letters,* London, 1941, p. 203.

** *The Complete Letters of Vincent van Gogh,* New York, 1958, Vol. II, p. 610.

An ambivalence of meaning has been discussed before (page 16), but now it takes on a new significance. Here is a field with its familiar overtones; and this same field hints at something else which is not an overtone. It transcends into an unnamed "beyond," of a demanding immediacy—a call to be heard, which is the more important message. Should we try to express it in so many words? I do not think it is necessary. We who are attuned to the language of the twentieth century know full well what came into the artist's vision.

This perception came upon him with growing insistence. In the drawing of Paris, the objects already have a peculiar mien. Take the two carts, for instance. While their practical purpose is obvious, their presence as such has an insistence which is not so plausible: that they are here, where they have been left standing, and in these positions—this is stated in a tone that makes them look strange—withdrawn and obtrusive at the same time. And once noticed here and there, this ambiguity will be felt everywhere, in the muteness of the buildings, in the brooding glow of semidarkness.

The period of Arles brings this "second sight" into the open, and now with a positive accent. Things no longer appear enigmatic; they are both intense and becalmed. Their other meaning chimes with their natural existence. It is moot to ask whether the luminosity is real or unreal. In the eyes of a portrait shine their factual color, the brightness of light, and the reflection of a transcendental radiance.

But in the drawing of Saint-Rémy (plate 147), a pressure rises in the furrowed soil, the crouching houses, the streaking rain, the clouds, and the twisted figure. Things begin to stir, the glow becomes overintense. The feverish lines attempt to hold and yet to release the fermentation. A pervasive

—I may say metaphysical—disquietude hangs over the landscape. It is a late work of the master, moving and disturbing.

It is almost incredible that the first and the third drawing are only three or four years apart. Van Gogh consummated the whole of his art within less than a decade. We know his tragic story—too well, perhaps, because we often confuse the man with the artist, and drag out personal motivations instead of looking for the impersonal and more relevant cause of his struggle. Van Gogh hears the knocking of a truth which seeks to come forth, always the same truth, whatever the subject. The pathetic effort to make it visible is the drama of his life.

Cézanne and Van Gogh shake off the intricacies and involvements of the nineteenth century. Their work tells us: "But one thing is needful." While the "one thing" is different for each, it addresses both of them as an imperative challenge, as a moral obligation. From now on, the quest of art feels a new responsibility.

There remains the discussion of contemporary landscape—but I shirk this task. A closed period of history is like a mountain range through which we have wandered. We can look back, can retrace our path, and recognize the high points. With present-day art, we are still in the woods. It is all around us, too close to our lives to be surveyed; or, rather, it *is* our life.

The reader will object that twentieth-century art has been at work for seventy years, that a good part of it is in no way "modern" any more, and that it has created a large number of eminent products which could answer our inquiry. No doubt, he is right; therefore, I must briefly state the reasons for my reluctance.

In this essay, I have attempted not to speak in generalities, but to interpret individual examples. By discussing the specific, I hope to show also the collective spirit of a period or of a nation. This method seems to be less productive when we come to the twentieth century. In the nineteenth century, art already tended to move in divergent directions. Contradictory trends succeeded each other; they even existed simultaneously. Since then, this tendency has taken on momentum. Expressions vary continuously and radically. Each major artist chooses an untrodden course. It is hard to determine whether and in which respect he is "typical."

Moreover, some artists feel compelled to supersede themselves without end, ever to be on the road, never at the goal. To take the measure of Picasso, for instance, one has to encompass his *oeuvre* from the early paintings and sculptures through its incessant transformations. Every few years, he discards his past definitions and finds new ones. But even those masters who pursue a more consistent line—Klee and Giacometti are examples—appear to experiment rather than to establish solutions. Contemporary art is exploratory —not through fickleness, but of necessity. We usually come to understand an artist of our times when we can study him in a sizable one-man show. The single examples in this book do not offer adequate documentation.

Still more perplexing is the fact that subject matter as such has lost significance. Like all other themes, landscape has become elusive. The traditional connotations—geography, history, nature, man—have changed or disappeared. Our imagination is steered in directions widely different from those

it took before. We see "through" the surface of the page; most contemporary works have a transparency of a new kind. We sense something else in, around, behind them. The drawing by Tobey (plate 155), while fairly allusive to nature (once we know the title), hardly *represents* it in the accepted sense; it refers to another realm. The "factual" view of Beckmann (plate 154) points to insights unconnected with landscape as such. Conversely, artifacts which are not supposed to represent nature may suggest colors and formations of nature—I believe such connotations can be found in some of Kandinsky's paintings.

The entire spiritual structure has been upset. When we ask ourselves what meaning the personality of a tree has (plate 151), what the identity of a mountain now is (plate 157), we realize that the answer lies far afield from the one we gave before. The objects do not fit into the categories of old, they hint at something else, they "transcend." But whence? Towards a meaning which defies rational definitions, to the "one thing" which haunted Van Gogh?

By the same token, the work of art has gained a new autonomy. In a way, it seems to form itself, to be independent of its maker who is often willing to let his hand move by its own impetus (plate 160), or to allow the ruler to take over (plate 150). In Mondrian's abstract compositions, the planes, intersections, and colors seek their equilibrium, they work it out through a logic of their own. Works of our century have a new motion and rhythm—a turnabout from the existence of the nineteenth.

Hence, they force the beholder into a different attitude. No longer is his position opposite the painting or drawing; he cannot scan it as an onlooker. Often, he has to read it like a written page, go along with the convolutions, the geometrical pattern or the transitions of color. In any case, he has to give up his place outside, to take a stance somewhere within, or to let himself be carried along in order to get the feel of the work. Yet such participation is not the "empathy" of old—what is it then?

These are questions, not answers. They may not satisfy the reader who will regret that the discussion stops short just at a period that interests him vitally. But he has his own convictions about modern art. He will compare my selections with the choices he would have made—probably entirely different ones. And this is as it should be. To see for ourselves, to make our own decisions and judgments, is our privilege and our duty.

THE DRAWINGS

Pisanello (Antonio Pisano)
Pisa 1395–1455 Rome

1. *Landscape with Two Churches*
c. 1440/50
Pen on red-grounded paper, 196×267 mm (7 5/8 × 10 3/8")*
The Louvre, Paris, No. 2280

BIBL. : B. Degenhart, *Antonio Pisanello,* Vienna, 1941, No. 141.
M. Fossi-Todorow, *I Disegni del Pisanello e della sua Cerchia,* Florence, 1966, No. 87.

The drawing is a rare example of landscape from the early *Quattrocento*. Probably it outlines the setting for a religious painting, but no finished work can be connected with it and the meaning of the large churches remains unexplained.

The subject is unusual for Pisanello. This would appear to be his only "pure" landscape. Mrs. Fossi-Todorow suggests that it may derive from a drawing by Jacopo Bellini who devised similar landscape models for his workshop. Pisanello met the Venetian at the court of the Este family in Ferrara in the 1440s.

Here is the spirit of the beginning Renaissance, just as it is in Pisanello's studies of heads and animals, and in his records of contemporary events. Sun, clouds, mountains, plain, buildings all over—a checkered world is brought alive by an alert and keen-witted narrator.

* *Measurements are given in millimeters and in inches, height preceding width.*

Sandro Botticelli
Florence 1444/45–1510 Florence

2. *Dante and Beatrice Rise Toward Heaven*
Pen over metalpoint on vellum, 320 × 474 mm (12 5/8 × 18 5/8″)
Kupferstichkabinett, East Berlin

BIBL. : L. Donati, *Il Botticelli e le Prime Illustrazioni della Divina Commedia,* Florence, 1962 (with complete Bibliography).
T. Yuen, "New Aspects of Botticelli's Late Works," *Marsyas,* XII, 1964/65, pp. 22 ff.

The drawing is one of the ninety-two illustrations to the *Divine Comedy,* commissioned by Lorenzo di Pierfrancesco de' Medici, which now are divided between the Vatican Library and the two Berlin Kupferstichkabinetts. They were believed to date from the early 1490s, but recent research points to the first decade of the sixteenth century (Yuen).

Beatrice and Dante are carried upward by the attraction of the Heavenly light (*Paradiso,* I, 46–54). To Botticelli and every Florentine, the place was well-known: the earthly Paradise, the summit of the mountain of Purgatory. He also knew the exact time: the morning of Wednesday, the 13th of April 1300.

Dante describes the many hues of color and light, the flowered meadow, the singing birds—it is one of the great passages in the *Divine Comedy* (*Purgatorio,* XXVIII). Botticelli does not aim to reproduce all that splendor, but concentrates upon the main features: the plateau with the circular river Lethe-Eunoë, the trees in their varied foliage *(la divina foresta spessa e viva),* and also the wind *(un' aura dolce, senza mutamento)* created by the movement of the celestial spheres.

See also Introduction, p. 15.

Central Italian Master

3. *Landscape with the Baptism of Christ and a Group of Horsemen*
c. 1500/1505
Pen and wash, 160×196 mm (6 5/16×7 11/16″); originally square; probably
   cut down on all sides
Uffizi, Florence, No. 402 P

BIBL. : O. H. Giglioli, "Disegni Italiani di Paese nella Galleria degli Uffizi," *Dedalo,* 1928/29,
   pp. 176 ff.

The purpose of this attractive sheet is unknown. The figure of God the
Father in the sky, the Baptism of Christ at the right, the military cortège
in the middle (the scene at the left is illegible) would indicate that it was
designed for a painting. No attribution has been attempted, to my knowledge; "da Raff.o da Urbino," as noted on the back, is untenable.

The trees are not as vigorous as Botticelli's. The landscape shows a mellower touch; the spread of mountains and valleys, the suggestion of atmosphere, point to the early years of the *Cinquecento.*

Leonardo da Vinci
Vinci 1452–1519 Cloux (France)

4. *The Valley of the Arno, near Florence*
    Inscribed by the artist "di di Santa Maria della neve addi 5 daghossto 1473"
      (day of Saint Mary of the Snow, August 5, 1473)
    Pen, 185 × 285 mm (7 5/16 × 11 3/16")
    Uffizi, Florence, No. 8 P

BIBL. : A. E. Popham, *The Drawings of Leonardo da Vinci*, New York, 1945, No. 253.
    B. Berenson, *I Disegni dei Pittori Fiorentini*, Milan, 1961, No. 1017.

Very likely the drawing is the first landscape done after nature. Leonardo, twenty-one years old, climbed a mountain near Florence and described the wide land from his vantage point. He must have had some pride in his achievement because he noted the date (Popham.)

A century and a half before, Petrarca had made his ascension of Mont Ventoux. On the summit, the world at his feet, he read in Saint Augustine's *Confessions* that "nothing counts except the soul." Leonardo's drawing reveals a different attitude to nature. With a scrutinizing mind, he studies the angular and curving formations, notes the differences of rocks and trees, of earth and water, the light glittering over the surfaces. Yet these are not isolated observations; "the pen has seldom been lifted from the paper" (Berenson), the exploration aims at the whole, and already is aware of principles which underlie all natural phenomena. This is why the landscape is of one piece, comprehensive, and strikes us with a singular intensity.

See also Introduction, p. 17.

Leonardo

Leonardo da Vinci

5. *An Alpine Valley with a Thunderstorm*
c. 1506
Red chalk, 190×150 mm (7 1/2×5 7/8″)
Royal Library, Windsor Castle, No. 12.409 (Reproduced by gracious permission of Her Majesty the Queen)

BIBL. : A. E. Popham, *op. cit.,* No. 261.
B. Berenson, *op. cit.,* No. 1251.
K. Clark, *A Catalogue of the Drawings of Leonardo da Vinci at Windsor Castle,* Cambridge, 1935; 2nd ed., London, 1968.

The sheet is done in red chalk, a medium Leonardo was the first to use without the addition of pen lines. The country resembles the Alpine valleys near Milan, where he lived at the court from 1483 to 1499.

During the years since the early landscape, Leonardo's explorations focused more and more on problems of science. This drawing was to him not a view, but a data sheet on the shading of clouds by light, on the gravity of air, or, most likely, on the formation of thunderstorms.

However, when applied to works of art, the term "science" has to be qualified. In the Renaissance, science was not yet a segregated field. The theoretical studies of Brunelleschi, Uccello, and others served their practical professions; the artist cannot be dissociated from the scientist. Facts of physics, perspective, and optics were expressed in works of art with such immediacy that one suspects they often were discovered through visual insight, and only afterwards underpinned by theory.

Therefore, we may enjoy Leonardo's drawing at sight, without thinking of a scientific intent. A dramatic play is enacted, of which the thunderstorm is the nucleus, with all the country sharing in the event: the high peaks above the turbulence, the declivity of the mountains, and the valley under the downpour or in sunlight.

See also Introduction, p. 16.

Leonardo da Vinci

6. *Study of Rock Formations*
c. 1508–11
Charcoal, 164 × 201 mm (6 7/16 × 7 7/8″)
Royal Library, Windsor Castle, No. 12.397 (Reproduced by gracious permission of Her Majesty the Queen)

BIBL. : J. P. Richter, *The Literary Works of Leonardo da Vinci,* Oxford, 1939.
A. E. Popham, *op. cit.,* No. 284 B.
B. Berenson, *op. cit.,* No. 1260.
K. Clark, *op. cit.*

"Mountains are made by the currents of rivers. Mountains are destroyed by rains and rivers" (Richter, 979). The sentences of Leonardo read like a comment on this sheet, and call attention to the water which flows under the rocks and gushes out at the bottom. Leonardo knows that the earth is in constant change, and he makes the evolution and its causes intelligible to the eye.

See also Introduction, p. 16.

Leonardo da Vinci

7. *Deluge*

c. 1515
Black chalk, 163 × 210 mm (6 3/8 × 8 1/4″)
Royal Library, Windsor Castle, No. 12.378 (Reproduced by gracious permission of Her Majesty the Queen)

BIBL. : J. P. Richter, *op. cit.*
A. E. Popham, *op. cit.,* No. 296.
J. Gantner, *Leonardos Visionen von der Sintflut und vom Untergang der Welt,* Bern, 1958.
B. Berenson, *op. cit.,* No. 1242.
K. Clark, *op. cit.*

The Deluge of the Bible and the end of the world on Judgment Day have been told time and again in Christian art, but always with regard to the fate of man. Seldom have they been presented as events pertinent to the history of the earth.

That the elements can get out of bounds and cause destruction was a logical consequence of Leonardo's train of thought. He frequently refers to this in his writings, as in a fictional letter (c. 1497) by an oriental magistrate who describes how flood, wind, and fire joined to lay waste a rich country in Armenia (Richter, 1337).

Water and its dangerous properties were studied by Leonardo in particular. The "Deluge" drawings date from his later years and are, in a sense, the ultimate in his preoccupations with nature. The sheet belongs to a series of ten, all evoking the destruction of the earth in progressing stages. This is not the Biblical Deluge. Noah's Ark would not have a chance to survive the assault from the waves and the swirling air. The catastrophe is total. At the left, the rocks are breaking up and are about to bury the town below. No doubt, Leonardo here envisions things to come. He recognizes the potential in nature's forces and thus the potential of the future. We look at the cataclysm with the fascination which we feel when suddenly confronted with a fateful event, even if, and perhaps just because, it is tragic. Disaster has a beauty of its own.

Fra Bartolommeo (Baccio della Porta)
Florence 1472–1517 Pian' di Mugnone

8. *Farm on the Slope of a Hill, with a Winepress Under an Arbor*
Pen, 222 × 292 mm (8 3/4 × 11 1/2")
The Cleveland Museum of Art. Dudley P. Allen Fund, Delia E. and L. E.
Holden Funds, and Gift of Hanna Fund, No. 57.498

BIBL. : R. W. Kennedy, "A Landscape Drawing by Fra Bartolommeo," *The Smith College Museum of Art Bulletin*, No. 39, 1959, pp. 8 ff.
I. Härth, "Zu Landschaftszeichnungen Fra Bartolommeos und seines Kreises," *Mitteilungen des Kunsthistorischen Institutes in Florenz*, IX, 1959, pp. 125 ff.
L. S. Richard, *The Bulletin of the Cleveland Museum*, No. 49, 1962, p. 172.
M. Winner, "Zwei Unbekannte Zeichnungen von Fra Bartolommeo und Albertinelli," *Studien aus dem Berliner Kupferstichkabinett Hans Möhle zugeeignet*, Berlin, 1966, pp. 21 ff.

From Fra Bartolommeo, few drawings of landscape were known until 1957 when an album of forty-one sheets appeared on the London market. The volume was assembled in the eighteenth century, but it is likely that most of the drawings were done at one time. They have relatively uniform sizes, the style is homogeneous, the views are varied. It has been proposed that the artist drew them on his journey to Venice in 1508, or after he moved to the monastery of Santa Maria Maddalena in the Val Mugnone, 1514; but this is conjectural. Also the relation of this drawing to a painting of 1509 is not close enough to supply a date.

Fra Bartolommeo may have had a practical purpose in mind with these records. Some were used literally in paintings done in his workshop.

Problems of date and use aside, the landscapes show a facet of the early sixteenth century which had so far remained little known. They transport the beholder into a countryside with small towns, water mills, old farms, amidst rocks and forests; he follows the travelers along the roads, he fairly breathes the limpid air. Fra Bartolommeo's art, blending clarity with grace, is purest "lingua toscana" at its most felicitous moment.

See also Introduction, p. 15.

Vittore Carpaccio
Venice 1460/65–c. 1526 Venice

9. *A Historical Scene in a Landscape*
c. 1495–1500
Pen over red chalk, 166 × 197 mm (6 1/2 × 7 3/4″)
Collection Duke of Devonshire, Chatsworth, No. 739 (Reproduced by permission of the Trustees of the Chatsworth Settlement)

BIBL. : J. Lauts, *Carpaccio Paintings and Drawings,* London, 1962, p. 266, No. 7.

Carpaccio's lives of saints belong to the most absorbing documents of the Venetian *Quattrocento*. The legends are divided into successive stages and read like chapters in a medieval chronicle. The scenes abound with bystanders and accessories which are as important as the leading actors.

Everything participates in this narration: the spectators at the sides, the barge nearing the shore, the horses in their varied movements, the monk's glance at the sky, and not least, the landscape. Much more than a setting, it is a partner in the story, and thus takes on the character of a specific locality.

The subject has been identified by Lauts: Cardinal Bessarion, the famed Greek scholar, delivers a reliquary to emissaries from Venice, for transmission to the Scuola della Carità. This happened in 1472, near Bologna, when Bessarion was on his way to France as papal legate. At the right is the Cardinal giving his benediction to the priest accepting the reliquary. The design seems to be intended for a painting, which however was not executed. It would have been Carpaccio's only representation of a contemporary event.

In Florence, the story would have been told in a different way. Here it has the stately and unhurried pace characteristic of Carpaccio and, later, Veronese.

Giorgione (Giorgio Barbarelli)
Castelfranco c. 1478–1510 Venice

10. *Landscape with a Walled Town and a Shepherd*
Red chalk, 203 × 290 mm (8 × 11 7/16")
Museum Boymans-van Beuningen, Rotterdam, No. I 485

BIBL. : H. Tietze and E. Tietze-Conrat, *The Drawings of the Venetian Painters,* New York, 1944, No. 709.

Giorgione's life-span was short, and his *oeuvre* small. That his art was of great consequence in the history of landscape is difficult to demonstrate here, as scarcely any drawings can be claimed as authentic. This "View of Castelfranco" is probably by his own hand, but some imagination is needed to appreciate the high quality of the sheet. It has suffered from rubbing, and the reproduction cannot render the subtle hue of the sanguine.

The drawing is perhaps a sketch for the background of a figure painting. The town may indeed be Giorgione's native Castelfranco—such walls are still standing there—but similar walls and towers appear also in Giovanni Bellini's paintings.

Here is a landscape quite different from Fra Bartolommeo's. The lone man in the foreground is set off from the country at his back; he even faces away from it. At the same time, he and the landscape are strikingly attuned to each other, and together compound the ambience which is peculiar to Venetian art.

There is also the difference of generations. While Giorgione is only slightly younger than Fra Bartolommeo, he speaks in terms of the sixteenth century. The ground has become solid, and supplies the basis for buildings and trees to stand upon, for the figure to sit upon. The progressive rise of terrain, the different heights of towers are articulated. Giorgione's landscape is "down to earth," still in a restrained way, but distinctly so.

Giulio Campagnola
Padua 1482–after 1515 Venice

11. *Mountainous Landscape with Buildings
    and Two Bearded Men in the Foreground*
Pen, 133 × 257 mm (5 1/4 × 10 1/4")
The Louvre, Paris, No. 4648

BIBL. : Tietzes, *op. cit.,* No. 579.
    U. Middeldorf, "Eine Zeichnung von Giulio Campagnola," *Festschrift für Martin Wack-
        ernagel,* Münster, 1958, pp. 141 ff.

The influence of Giorgione on his contemporaries is evident from the large number of "Giorgionesque" works, amongst them those of Giulio Campagnola. This drawing reflects Giorgione at a more advanced stage than in the preceding example. Again, the tone is set by the relationship of persons and landscape, but the two heavyset men and the well-furnished country now provide a richer consonance.

This is a printmaker's design. The short lines and dots embroider a pattern of dark and light which will appeal especially to the amateur of prints. Giulio devised a new technique in engraving to achieve a painterly surface. All the contours on the drawing are pricked for transfer to the plate, but the engraving was made only later, by the younger Campagnola, Domenico, and with a significant change: by that time, about 1517, the "philosophers" with their hermetic urn had gone out of fashion, and were replaced by a foursome of young musical shepherds. Also the trees above them were altered to conform to a modern style—that of Titian.

Titian (Tiziano Vecellio)
Pieve di Cadore c. 1485/88–1576 Venice

12. *A Group of Trees*
Inscribed "Giorgione" by a later hand
c. 1516
Pen, 217 × 319 mm (8 9/16 × 12 9/16")
The Metropolitan Museum of Art, New York City. Rogers Fund,
   No. 08.227.38

BIBL. : Tietzes, *op. cit.,* No. 1943.
   J. Bean and F. Stampfle, Exhibition Catalogue, *Drawings from New York Collections, The Italian Renaissance,* New York, 1965, No. 58.

As in the case of Giorgione, experts have become cautious in ascribing drawings to Titian. There exist a handful of figure sketches for paintings, but hardly any landscapes qualify. To get the measure of Titian in landscape, one has to depend on his paintings such as the *Sacred and Profane Love,* or the *Pardo Venus.*

This group of trees, however, stands out in quality and has a claim to the master's own hand. The trunks are set off against the compact foliage, and range with a freedom that recalls Titian's human figures of the same time. Together, the trees embody an aggregate strength akin to that of the Apostles in the *Assunta* (Frari, Venice).

Titian gives a new turn to landscape. He packs things with an energy and weight beyond Giorgione's "solidity." How the ground swells, how the trees rise and spread—they bespeak a fervor (may we say an "idealism"?) which exceeds their material existence.

The drawing was used in a woodcut after Titian (*The Sacrifice of Abraham,* Passavant VI, 223.3). The somewhat blurred pen lines suggest that a counterproof has been made for the printmaker—which would corroborate the attribution (Bean). The connection with the print also supplies the approximate date.

METROPOLITAN MVSEVM OF ART NEW YORK

Giorgione

Titian (?)

13. *Landscape with a Fortified Castle*
1510/20
Pen, 216 × 347 mm (8 1/2 × 13 5/8″)
Musée Bonnat, Bayonne, No. 1323

BIBL. : Tietzes, *op. cit.,* No. 1875.
    J. Bean, *Les Dessins Italiens de la Collection Bonnat,* Paris, 1960, No. 171.

This landscape, too, appears in a woodcut (*Landscape with a Milkmaid,* Passavant, VI, 96), but the drawing may not be by the master's own hand. The handwriting is somewhat timid and painstaking (note the foliage), and things lack the "body" of the preceding sheet.

The invention, however, is Titian's, and shows why his landscapes made such an impact and set a new standard. The country, in its staggered rise, accentuated by the trees and the stalwart buildings, is a full-fledged organism, self-sufficient like a story with human figures. The scene is local; these are the Alpine foothills which Titian remembered from his youth in Val Cadore. Yet it also suggests a concept of greater consequence, that of the earth, of its extent and greatness. The beholder is in the surrounding of a specific region; at the same time, he is awed by a commanding image.

Domenico Campagnola
Venice 1500–after 1552

14. *Landscape with Two Figures*
Pen, 198 × 285 mm (7 3/4 × 11 1/4")
Kupferstichkabinett, Staatliche Museen, West Berlin, No. 434

BIBL. : H. Tietze and E. Tietze-Conrat, "Domenico Campagnola's Graphic Art," *Print Collectors Quarterly,* 1939, pp. 311 ff. and 445 ff.
Tietzes, *op. cit.,* No. 421.

Through the graphic work of Domenico Campagnola, Titian's type of landscape was widely circulated and became a major influence, south and north of the Alps. It was to become one of Bruegel's sources, and later a factor in the formation of "classical" landscape. It will even reappear in some of Rembrandt's etchings.

Somewhat paradoxically, history was made by an artist whose stature is relatively small. Domenico's engravings and woodcuts—mostly dated as early as 1517/18—clearly reflect Titian, but they are often awkward in technique and composition. They do not seem to reproduce drawings of the great master literally, and rather look like variations on his style.

A number of drawings ascribed to Campagnola (many attributions are controversial) are higher in quality than the prints. This page shows the vigorous, if somewhat indifferent, hatching of a design for a woodcut. The crossed trunks of the trees, the complex of large old houses, expertly ranged, the two men walking through the rugged and homely country—all are elements taken from Titian, though here more ostentatious and forced.

Polidoro da Caravaggio
Caravaggio 1490/1500–1543(?) Messina

15. *Landscape with a Crouching Figure*
Brown wash, heightened with white, on brown paper, 204×270 mm
(8 1/16×10 5/8")
Uffizi, Florence, No. 498 P

BIBL. : A. Chatelet, "Two Landscape Drawings by Polidoro da Caravaggio," *Burlington Magazine,*
1954, pp. 181 ff.
A. R. Turner, "Two Landscapes in Renaissance Rome," *Art Bulletin,* 1961, pp. 275 ff.
J. A. Gere, "A Landscape Drawing by Polidoro da Caravaggio," *Master Drawings,* I,
1963, pp. 43 ff.
A. R. Turner, *The Vision of Landscape in Renaissance Italy,* Princeton, 1966.
A. Marabottini, *Polidoro da Caravaggio,* Rome, 1969, Vol. II (Catalogo dei Disegni), No. 6.

Our examples of Italian sixteenth-century landscape are scanty. For a good reason: landscape did not then have the same status in Italy as in the North; easel paintings, in which landscape is dominant, are rare. It was a theme acceptable for prints and the adornment of walls—two divergent uses, with different aspects of nature. The development, the crosscurrents, the foreign influences have been explored in A. R. Turner's imaginative book. A few landscape drawings have been ascribed to Polidoro who worked in Rome from about 1517 to 1527. His major activity was the decoration of facades in *grisaille,* and this sheet, done with the brush, is perhaps connected with such work. Dark and light portions are strongly contrasted, distance is suggested by a separation of planes—all this would be effective in a large fresco.

The weird mood allures and puzzles. Who is the pathetic woman? A penitent Magdalene? Are the buildings in ruins? Is it night or day? The mystification seems to be intentional.

It should be mentioned that there are other landscapes by Polidoro which are quite matter-of-fact (Gere).

Albrecht Dürer
Nuremberg 1471–1528 Nuremberg

16. *Study of Rocks, with a Castle and a Wanderer*
c. 1493/94
Pen, 225 × 316 mm (8 7/8 × 12 7/16″)
Albertina, Vienna, No. 3055

BIBL. : F. Winkler, *Die Zeichnungen Albrecht Dürers,* Berlin, 1936–39. No. 57.
E. Panofsky, *Albrecht Dürer,* 3rd ed., Princeton, 1948, No. 1372.

In turning to an earlier period and to a northern country, one has to adjust to a different standard. The crowded rocks bring to mind the narrow alleys and the overhanging houses of a Gothic town. Yet Dürer breaks away from these confines and opens up a wide and visionary country.

This is an early sheet, but it already bespeaks the genius of the master who, for a short while, brought German art to supranational greatness. Winkler, stating that the drawing is difficult to date, sets the outside limits wide apart: 1492 and 1497. Dürer changed a great deal in those five years. Panofsky's "1493/94" appears convincing; and Winkler himself places the reproduction amongst the works which precede Dürer's departure to Venice in 1494.

See also Introduction, p. 17.

Albrecht Dürer

17. *A Quarry and Trees*
Inscription added by a later hand
c. 1495/97
Watercolor, 214×168 mm (8 7/16×6 5/8″)
Kupferstichkabinett, Staatliche Museen, West Berlin, No. 15338

BIBL. : Winkler, *op. cit.,* No. 111.

In a selection of Dürer's landscapes, those in watercolor and gouache cannot be missed. They are little marvels of perception and lucidity, fascinating by their strength and subtlety. Part of them are highly elaborated, and paintings in miniature rather than drawings; the many-hued tints sparkle on the paper like precious stones. Color reproductions usually are incorrect at some point of the spectrum. Therefore a less polychrome sheet is illustrated here to give a foretaste of originals.

Dürer used this technique only for objects whose materials and colors attracted him: animals, their skins, feathers or shells, plants, and landscapes. The latter begin with views taken in and around Nuremberg in 1493/94; a larger group from the journey to Venice follows; finally, there is a series done between 1495 and 1500 to which this watercolor belongs. After that time, Dürer does not seem to have made landscapes in color—unless the famous *Large Piece of Turf* is classed as such.

No doubt, the master produced the pages for his own satisfaction. He held on to them—as to most of his drawings—and used several of the motifs in his prints. The bare trees reappear about two decades later, in the upper right corner of *Knight; Death and Devil,* where their bristly shapes beautifully conform with the sharp lineament and austere character of the engraving. While the trees were limned meticulously, with very fine brushes, the rocks were painted only broadly and remained unfinished. Dürer must have visited the quarry of calcareous stone frequently during a certain period. He depicted it in various drawings and watercolors, amongst them one that shows the entire cliff (Winkler, No. 110).

Albrecht Dürer

18. *Forest Spring with Saint Paul and Saint Anthony*
1501/2
Pen and black ink, 186×185 mm (7 5/16×7 1/4")
Kupferstichkabinett, Staatliche Museen, West Berlin, No. 3867

BIBL. : Winkler, *op. cit.,* No. 182.

Two sections of the sheet are completed in hatching lines, the rest is only outlined. We can observe how the master deepens the shade between the trees, how he embeds the spring-well in the ground and builds stones and steps around it. Even at this unfinished stage, the landscape suggests the comfortable ambience of a clearing in the dense forest.

The drawing was done in preparation for a woodcut representing the meeting of the hermit Saints Anthony and Paul (Bartsch, 107). The raven which brings Saint Paul his daily loaf of bread is just arriving. In the woodcut the figures are larger and more prominent, they are placed not within, but at the edge of the forest; the format is upright.

The sheet is from the same time as the well-known *Hare* in the Albertina (1502; Winkler, No. 248).

See also Introduction, p. 17.

Albrecht Dürer

19. *View of Heroldsberg*
Signed and dated 1510
Pen, 211 × 263 mm (8 5/16 × 10 3/8″)
Musée Bonnat, Bayonne

BIBL. : Winkler, *op. cit.,* No. 481.

To know the name of a locality adds to our enjoyment. This is Heroldsberg, a hamlet near Nuremberg, where relatives of Willibald Pirckheimer, the friend of Dürer, owned an estate. The drawing probably is an elaboration of a preliminary sketch from nature (Winkler).

It is a rare satisfaction to witness a medieval world which is so far removed from ours and does not exist any more. We scan it for signs of life and, indeed, we find a few people around, a stork in the air, and smoke rising from a chimney. Yet Dürer also tells something which goes beyond our historical curiosity and concerns us directly: his landscape conveys the strength and solidity of the earth, and the beauty of all the things which stand on it, be they natural or man-made.

See also Introduction, p. 18.

Albrecht Dürer

20. *The Port of Antwerp*
Inscribed by Dürer "Antorff" and dated 1520
Pen, 213 × 283 mm (8 3/8 × 11 1/4")
Albertina, Vienna, No. 3165

BIBL. : Winkler, *op. cit.,* No. 821.

The famous drawing is one of the many which Dürer did during his journey to the Netherlands in 1520/21.

Here a maximum of clarity has been attained. Observe the layout of the page, the sureness of the contours, the economy of line—a modern critic may speak of "geometrization."

Reproductions have a sly way of cheating. While they pretend to tell the truth, they blur the impact which only the work itself can make. Seen in the original, this drawing gives a stronger suggestion of space: space above the ground, between the masts and the roofs, and also behind the buildings. More important, things are not merely well-coordinated. The massive, upright buildings, the empty square and water, the small figures—they actively band together. There is a note of immediacy and suspense which is the essence of the drawing.

See also Introduction, p. 18.

Albrecht Dürer

21. *Fortification Between a Rocky Mountain and the Sea*
c. 1527
Pen, 213 × 202 mm (8 3/8 × 7 15/16")
Biblioteca Ambrosiana, Milan

BIBL. : Winkler, *op. cit.,* No. 942.

The drawing has suffered from foxing. The contrast with the early mountain is implicit in every stroke. Observe how expressive the oblique drop has become, how the vertical rises from the horizontal of the sea, how the minute objects are gauged at the height of the rock.

The pen seems to size up and to shape the mountain, as a chisel carves a statue from the block. Each line is conscious of the entire structure. Philip Melanchthon, the humanist, relates that Dürer told him: "As a young man, I liked florid and multiform paintings and I enjoyed looking at such variety in my work. After I got old, I began to see nature's simple face, and I recognized that this simplicity is art's greatest virtue."*

The landscape is freely invented. Very likely the design is connected with Dürer's "Treatise on Fortification" of 1527, dedicated to Ferdinand of Hungary, who was preparing to defend his kingdom against the Turks.

See also Introduction, p. 18.

* In a letter of Melanchthon to Prince Georg of Anhalt-Dessau, December 17, 1546 (H. Rupprich, *Dürer, Schriftlicher Nachlass,* Berlin, 1956, Vol. I, No. 143, p. 289).

Lucas Cranach the Elder
Kronach 1472–1553 Weimar

22. *Angels in Clouds, a Landscape with Buildings*
(from Prayer Book of Emperor Maximilian, folio 61 recto)
Signed with winged dragon and dated 1515
Pen in red and brown on vellum, 278 × 194 mm (10 15/16 × 7 5/8″)
Bayerische Staatsbibliothek, Munich

BIBL. : Panofsky, *op. cit.*, pp. 182 ff.
J. Rosenberg, *Die Zeichnungen Lucas Cranach d. Ä.*, Berlin, 1960, No. 26.

The Emperor Maximilian, "the last knight," who reigned from 1493–1519, was a dedicated, if somewhat erratic, patron of the arts. One of his many projects was a printed prayer book, with margins illustrated in woodcut. It was to vie with the illuminated manuscripts of old times and be presented to the Knights of the Order of Saint George. Ten copies of the text were printed on vellum, and the quires of one copy distributed to various artists who filled the margins with their drawings. Most of them were made by Dürer, the rest by Altdorfer, Baldung, Breu, Cranach and one unidentified draftsman. The plan was not carried to completion, but the copy with the drawings still exists. One part is in Munich, the other in Besançon.

It seems that the artists were given freedom to fill the pages as they wished. Cranach decorated one quire, mostly with animals: storks, apes, and his familiar stags. Unlike Dürer's, his designs have no reference to the prayers and psalms of the text. This sheet is the only landscape amongst his eight pages, and the only one in two colors, the buildings and angels in red, the plants brown. Such quaint landscapes appear also in his paintings, be it a Holy Family or a nymph at a fountain. The mossy larches, the churches and castles could set the stage for an old German fairy tale.

It is assumed that Dürer devised the combination of the printed page with a figured margin. Curiously, it did not find any following then and became a common practice only in the nineteenth century.

Gratio·

Protege domine popu-
lum tuū et apostoloꝛū
tuoꝛū Petri et Pauli: et alio-
rum apostolorum patrocinio
confidentem:perpetua defen-
sione conserua· Per·

De sanctis Gratio·

Omnes sancti tui quesu-
mus domine nos vbi-
ꝙ adiuuent:vt dum eoꝛū me-
rita recolimus:patrocinia sen-
tiamus: et pacem tuam no-
stris tōcede temporibus: et ab

Hans Baldung Grien
Schwäbisch-Gmünd 1484/85–1545 Strasbourg

23. *A View of Strasbourg from the Cathedral*
(from Baldung Sketchbook, folio 20 verso and 21 recto)
Inscription "HGB" added by another hand
1520/25
Silverpoint, 205 × 302 mm (8 1/16 × 11 7/8")
Kunsthalle, Karlsruhe

BIBL. : C. Koch, *Die Zeichnungen Hans Baldung Griens,* Berlin, 1941, No. 224.

Sketchbooks have been a part of the artists' equipment since the Middle Ages, but few have come down to us intact. When drawings became a marketable commodity, it was more profitable to sell the pages singly. Thus, a complete sketchbook by a major artist is a rare treasure, even if, like this one which was reconstructed by a descendant of Baldung, it is not in the original condition.

Among other notations, the book contains views of Strasbourg, all made from the platform of the Münster. This drawing spreads over two pages, and shows a central section of the city. Most of the buildings no longer exist; the layout of the streets, however, is much the same today.

Strictly speaking, this is not a landscape, but it presents such a revealing likeness of a Gothic town that I could not resist adding it to the selection. We are carried back five hundred years, when cities were small (Strasbourg then had a population of about twenty-five thousand), churches and trees numerous, and the open fields just beyond the walls.

Albrecht Altdorfer
Regensburg c. 1480–1538 Regensburg

24. *A Forest Interior with the Dead Pyramus*
C. 1511
Pen in black and white ink, on blue-grounded paper, 213 × 156 mm
  (8 3/8 × 6 1/4")
Kupferstichkabinett, Staatliche Museen, West Berlin, No. 83

BIBL. : F. Winzinger, *Albrecht Altdorfer, Zeichnungen,* Munich, 1952, No. 27.

In southeastern Germany, there developed a distinctive school (partly under Cranach's influence) in which landscape became a favorite subject, more so than on the Rhine and Main. In fact, the only *paintings* of landscape without any figures that are known from the early sixteenth century are by Altdorfer, the chief master of the "Danube School."

Most of Altdorfer's drawings are "chiaroscuros": a dark color is applied on the paper (the sponging can be noticed in the reproduction) as ground to the white and black of the pen. Chiaroscuros appear more complete than black-on-white drawings, and probably were valued as finished works.

The sheet illustrated here leads us into the interior of a dense and somber forest. The corpse lies among the dead wood as if it belonged there. Indeed, nature seems to have taken over, and a willful element seems to guide the convoluted lines. Do we meet an extravagant and disturbing streak in German art? I do not think so, but the balance has been tilted in favor of a more arbitrary aspect; a step has been taken away from Dürer, and also beyond Dürer. Altdorfer is more partial; not in subject matter—his *Battle of Alexander* (Munich) is worldwide—but in intent. He makes nature into a specific category; landscape now becomes an "institution," to use Gombrich's terminology.

Art historians interpret Altdorfer in widely differing ways, from the "gemütlich" to the "demonic."

Wolf Huber

Feldkirch 1480/85–1553 Passau

25. *Mondsee and Schafberg in the Salzkammergut*
Signed "W. H." and dated 1510
Pen, 127 × 205 mm (5 × 8 1/16")
Germanisches Museum, Nuremberg, No. 218

BIBL. : P. Halm, "Die Landschaftszeichnungen des Wolfgang Huber," *Münchner Jahrbuch für Bildende Kunst,* N. F., VII, 1930, No. 32.

Huber is the other prominent master of the Danube School. This landscape has a different character. It is quite factual; Huber saw it on a journey through the Austrian Alps and probably recorded it right on the spot.

The penmanship is striking. The artist defines the contours with an expert hand and builds them into a lucid whole where each large or small feature—even signature and date—has its place. He did the drawing at a young age, but with the sureness and economy accruing from the graphic tradition of a hundred years.

The country is viewed from a low vantage point and lies half-hidden behind the bridge and the pollard willows. Yet it demands to be read in three dimensions, and not only from the front. A wide space is spread out under the sky, lake and mountains describe a big circle, and one is aware of the land all around them. Within the larger context, the locality takes on a personal face.

Wolf Huber

26. *The Danube in Austria, near Krems*
Signed "W. H." and dated 1529
Pen on reddish-grounded paper, 224×317 mm (8 3/4×12 1/2")
Kupferstichkabinett, Staatliche Museen, West Berlin, No. 12303

BIBL. : P. Halm, *op. cit.,* No. 8.

Here is the Wachau, halfway between Passau and Vienna. Huber's style has changed since the earlier drawing; he takes a higher viewpoint and describes the beautiful country in all its riches.

Had he seen in the meantime Flemish "world landscapes," or Venetian woodcuts with Titianesque mountains? These are moot questions, and not too relevant, for the German gives his own version of nature. He is more effusive than a Netherlander; and his rising hills and castles, the earth under the beaming light, betray a feeling for things and their behavior that is foreign to the Italian master.

Urs Graf
Solothurn 1485–1528 Basel(?)

27. *Castles on a Crag*
Signed "VG" and dated 1514
Pen in black ink, 225 × 158 mm (8 7/8 × 6 1/4")
Öffentliche Kunstsammlung, Basel, No. K. 53

BIBL. : H. Koegler, *Beschreibendes Verzeichnis der Basler Handzeichnungen des Urs Graf,* Basel, 1926,
No. 53.
E. Major and E. Gradmann, *Urs Graf,* London, 1947, No. 72.

In the Germany of the Renaissance, little distinction was made between artist and artisan. Urs Graf was painter, woodcutter, goldsmith, and die cutter for the mint of Basel. He had a further profession, that of a mercenary soldier. It was a common, sometimes profitable métier of the Swiss, and one that suited Graf perfectly because he was a roguish character who frequently got himself into trouble.

His temper shows in his art as well. The drawings, many of them of lansquenets and their female companions, are dashed with free but sure pen strokes.

Only two landscapes are known, both from 1514. This one is thoroughly and purposely imaginary. It virtually bursts with energy. The way in which the towering mountain lifts the castle upward recalls flamboyant Late Gothic architecture. There is a good deal of sophistication in German graphic art, and it increases as the sixteenth century proceeds. The handling becomes more calligraphic; linear pattern takes the upper hand. Other European nations outgrew that stage, but to Germany a second flowering was denied for a long time to come.

Augustin Hirschvogel
Nuremberg 1503–1553 Vienna

28. *The Castle of Neuburg*
c. 1543
Pen in two tones of ink over silverpoint, 181 × 307 mm (7 1/8 × 12 1/8″)
Kupferstichkabinett, Staatliche Museen, West Berlin, No. 4717

BIBL. : A. Schmitt, "Eine Ansicht von Neuburg und der Donau aus dem 16. Jahrhundert,"
Berliner Museen, Berichte aus den ehem. Preussischen Kunstsammlungen, N.F., IV, 1954,
pp. 8 ff.

Neuburg is situated on the Upper Danube. In Hirschvogel's time, it was the seat of a Count Palatine.

The town is seen from the north bank of the river. Hirschvogel describes it meticulously; one can even distinguish the Renaissance structures which the Count built. In reality, castle and churches stand wider apart; the artist liked them better crammed together. In contrast, the willows in front are loosely spread and suggest a pleasurable spaciousness to which the little man, who looks with us across the Danube, adds his cheerful note. Not without reason, a darker ink has been used for the foreground.

The work shows the high level which German draftsmanship still maintained at mid-century.

Jan van Scorel

Scorel near Alkmaar 1495–1562 Utrecht

29. *A Castle upon Rocks* (verso)
Signed on recto "IO SCO"
c. 1520
Pen, 207 × 155 mm (8 1/4 × 6 1/16")
British Museum, London, No. 1909.1.9.7

Our first example from the Netherlands is by a Dutchman, a painter of altarpieces and portraits. Scorel was one of the early "Romanists" who studied the new canon of the Renaissance in Rome. The pilgrimage of artists to Italy had started about 1500. It was to last for centuries and fertilize the South no less than the North.

Not many drawings by Scorel are extant, and the few of landscapes have little connection with the painted work.

This sheet will illustrate the difference between the Netherlandish and the German approach. The contrast to Urs Graf's castle-mountain is striking indeed: no sweeping flourishes, but a controlled line. The pen moves slowly and with deliberation; it is attentive to the varied shapes, and fashions them into a coherent texture upon which a soft light seems to play.

The castle may be a record from Scorel's journey, started in 1518, which led him through Carinthia. He traveled as far as the Holy Land and finally came to Rome.

The other side of the page shows a mountain with a bridge.

Maerten van Heemskerck
Heemskerk 1498–1574 Haarlem

30. *The South Corner of the Palatine; In the Background the Colosseum*
(from Heemskerck Sketchbook II, folio 55 recto)
1532/36
Pen, 282×237 mm (11 1/16×9 5/16″)
Kupferstichkabinett, Staatliche Museen, West Berlin

BIBL. : C. Huelsen and H. Egger, *Die Römischen Skizzenbücher von Maarten van Heemskerck,* Berlin, 1913.

Heemskerck, a Dutchman like his teacher Scorel, resided in Rome from 1532 to 1536. Unlike Scorel, he was an avid recorder of facts. He made hundreds of sketches after Roman antiquities and Renaissance works. The former are preserved, mainly in two large volumes now in Berlin.

These contain many *vedute,* set down with faithful accuracy. One would assume that Heemskerck intended his views for prints, but only the one reproduced here was used in an engraving, and that much later, in a series published in 1561.

Yet the drawing is not only an archeological document, it reflects a Netherlander's concept of landscape at that time. The ruins stand with a somewhat pompous grandeur, their gravity relieved by a diffuse atmosphere; they combine into a narrative description, in which the little figures have their natural place.

Mathys Cock
Antwerp c. 1509–1548 Antwerp

31. *An Inlet of the Sea, with Rocky Peninsulas and a Harbor*
Dated 1538
Pen, 192 × 288 mm (7 1/2 × 11 3/8″)
Staatliche Graphische Sammlung, Munich, No. 34491

BIBL. : T. Muchall-Viebrook, *Old Master Drawings,* VI, No. 22, Sept. 1931, p. 29.

The mainstream of early Netherlandish painting was in Flanders; here landscape had a long tradition. It played an essential role in religious subjects; and this, paradoxically, may be the reason why it was slow in becoming independent. Patinir (d. 1524) is considered the first painter of pure landscape. He spreads out a wide and varied country which reaches far to a high horizon. Lacking any drawings which can safely be ascribed to him, we show one by a follower. It displays the ambition of the sixteenth century to convey a comprehensive image. Is it "pure" landscape? As in Patinir's paintings, the story is indispensable. Take the lively traffic on water and shore away and the scenery will become vacant and indifferent.

Those were the times when the galleons of the explorers and conquerors cast off for distant lands; an embarkation then may have looked not far different from this one. No doubt, people were curious to see strange countries and seagoing vessels, and such drawings served for the engravings which Jerome Cock, the brother of Mathys, published in Antwerp.

See also Introduction, p. 19.

1538

Jerome Cock

Antwerp c. 1510–1570 Antwerp

32. *The Palatine Hill in Rome*
Signed "H Cok"
Pen and ink of various dilutions, 222 × 324 mm (8 3/4 × 12 3/4")
Prentenkabinet, Rijksuniversiteit, Leiden. Collection Welcker, No. AW 1185

BIBL. : F. W. H. Hollstein, *Dutch and Flemish Etchings, Engravings and Woodcuts*, Vol. IV, Amsterdam, n. d.
Exhibition Catalogue, *Het Vroege Landschap*, Stedelijke Museum De Lakenhal, Leiden, 1966/67, No. 34.

We know Jerome Cock mainly as a publisher of prints after designs by his brother Mathys, Pieter Bruegel, and many others. It is assumed that Jerome himself engraved some of his large output.

There are a number of drawings by his own hand. This south slope of the Palatine probably was drawn during Jerome's stay in Rome, about 1546–48. It still reflects Patinir's spreading landscapes with their copious narrative, yet it is less arbitrary than it seems. Rome looked that way before she was built up into a coherent city toward 1600. Several of the ruins can be identified. Reality and fantasy are mixed, however, to entertain as well as to instruct the beholder.

The same locality, further amplified and embellished, appears in the etched series of Roman buildings which Cock issued in 1562 (Hollstein, p. 36).

Pieter Bruegel the Elder
Breda(?) c. 1525-1569 Brussels

33. *A Fortified Town with Mountains and the Sea*
Signed "p brueghel" and dated 1553
Pen and ink of various dilutions, 237×335 mm (9 5/16×13 1/4")
British Museum, London, No. 1909.4.6.1.

BIBL. : Ch. de Tolnay, *The Drawings of Pieter Bruegel the Elder,* New York, 1952, No. 7.
O. Benesch, "Charles de Tolnay, Die Zeichnungen Pieter Bruegels," *Kunstchronik,* 1953,
pp. 76 ff.
L. Münz, *Bruegel, The Drawings,* London, 1961, No. 3.

The earliest known works of Bruegel are landscape drawings.

The first of his "Large Landscapes" dates from 1552, the year when the young artist departed for Italy. He returned to Antwerp before 1555, and continued to draw such vistas throughout the decade. A use for prints may have been intended; in fact, Jerome Cock issued a series of engravings in 1558 where some motifs of the drawings reappear.

Such a purpose, though not carried out, is likely for this sheet. It displays a far-reaching panorama, a wealth of fanciful detail—just what would satisfy the curiosity for foreign lands and cities. Bruegel offers more; he proliferates and spreads the mountains and buildings, shapes earth and clouds with an imagination and intensity unknown in previous world landscapes (see plate 31).

See also Introduction, p. 19.

Pieter Bruegel the Elder

34. *Mountain Landscape with a River Valley*
Signed "P. Bruegel"
c. 1555
Pen and ink of various dilutions, 350×435 mm (13 3/4×17 1/4")
Pierpont Morgan Library, New York City, No. 1952.25

BIBL. : F. Stampfle, in *Third Annual Report to the Fellows of the Morgan Library,* New York, 1952,
       pp. 64 ff.
       O. Benesch, *op. cit.*
       Ch. de Tolnay, *Bulletin Musées Royaux des Beaux-Arts,* Brussels, 1960, pp. 3 ff.
       L. Münz, *op. cit.,* No. 21.

This largest, and one of the most grandiose of the "Large Landscapes" became known only recently, after its long slumber in a private British collection. The style suggests a later date than that of the previous drawing.

It stands to reason that Bruegel did not execute such drawings while on the road, but after his return, when he had the time and facilities to elaborate the large sheets.

Only few can be pinned to known localities; the Morgan drawing is perhaps one of these. Benesch thought one could recognize the Upper Rhine, in the Swiss Canton of Grisons, with the castle Jörgenberg and the village Ruis. While it is gratifying to know where we are, the scope clearly exceeds a topographical intent. It is a joy to roam through the artist's country; one makes a new discovery at each visit. Yet all the particulars are embedded in a "world"—the term is meant in a physical as well as a conceptual sense. None in this group of landscapes shows Rome and the ancient monuments that had attracted Bruegel's predecessors. Wild mountains, rivers, and lakes, isolated dwellings meant more to him. It is significant that his travels took him beyond Rome, as far as Sicily.

See also Introduction, p. 19.

Pieter Bruegel the Elder

35. *Castle with Round Towers; at the Left a River*
Signed "Bruegel" and dated 1561
Pen and ink of various dilutions, 143 × 190 mm (5 5/8 × 7 1/2")
Kupferstichkabinett, Staatliche Museen, West Berlin, No. 5765

BIBL. : Ch. de Tolnay, *The Drawings of Pieter Bruegel the Elder*, No. 36.
L. Münz, *op. cit.*, No. 38.

A group of drawings, dated between 1559 and 1561, is markedly at variance with the "Large Landscapes." The format is smaller, the layout more compact, the motifs picturesque. Probably the sheets were intended for a series of engravings (or etchings?) in a novel style. The graphic quality differs from Bruegel's earlier as well as later drawings; the short strokes and dots seem to demonstrate to the engraver how to produce a painterly effect.

Indeed, these landscapes give the illusion of a glimmering atmosphere that goes beyond anything known before. They have been called "pre-Impressionist"—which, I believe, misinterprets their scope. Their sparkle is not merely optical, but pregnant with meaning.

Münz and Tolnay stress symbolic connotations: rocks and water indicate obstacles and perils, light and vegetation suggest the universal power of nature. Perhaps some day, such hidden allusions, if any, will be decoded; but even at face value, the drawings are singularly vivid and suggestive. There is something mysterious and labyrinthic in this sheet; one would think that the castle knows more than the beholder does.

A comparison with Scorel's castle-mountain (plate 29) shows at a glance that Bruegel gave a new personality to landscape. By hindsight, we accept this for granted, but it was truly the "invention" of a genius.

Pieter Bruegel the Elder

36. *Marine Landscape, with a View of Antwerp*
c. 1562
Pen and ink of various dilutions, 205 × 300 mm (7 7/8 × 11 3/4")
Collection Count Antoine Seilern, London

BIBL. : Ch. de Tolnay, *op. cit.,* No. 1.
Count A. Seilern, *Flemish Paintings and Drawings at 56 Princes Gate, London,* 1955, No. 11.
C. Kreuzberg, "Zur Seesturm-Allegorie Bruegels," *Festschrift Wilhelm Fränger,* Berlin, 1960, pp. 33 ff.
L. Münz, *op. cit.,* No. 50.

Bodies of rivers, lakes, or sea appear in many drawings of the master, but this is the only one where the water is all-important. Therefore it is not easy to place the sheet within his *oeuvre*. In penmanship, it is comparable to the drawing of "Spes" from 1559 (Münz, No. 145), but in intent it is close to the late painting of a sea storm in Vienna.

Count Seilern raises the question whether the sea and the storm-tossed boats have an allegorical meaning. The same problem was discussed by Kreuzberg in connection with the Vienna painting. There the sky, lighting up behind the church tower on the horizon, seems to symbolize the beacon of salvation above the dark perilous waters of life.

See also Introduction, p. 20.

Master of the Small Landscapes

37. *Street in a Village*
   c. 1555/59
   Pen, 129×397 mm (5 1/16×15 5/8")
   The Metropolitan Museum of Art, New York City. Rogers Fund,
      No. 06.1042.6

BIBL. : A. E. Popham, *Catalogue of Drawings by Dutch and Flemish Artists in the British Museum,*
   London, 1932, Vol. V, p. 144.
   J. C. J. Bierens de Haan, *L'Oeuvre gravé de Cornelis Cort,* The Hague, 1948, p. 216.
   E. Haverkamp Begemann, *Willem Buytewech,* Amsterdam, 1959, p. 38.
   W. Stechow, *Dutch Landscape Painting of the Seventeenth Century,* London, 1966, p. 16.

The drawing belongs to a series which Jerome Cock published in print in 1559 and 1561. Formerly it was ascribed to Bruegel, but recently it has been given to Cornelis Cort, whose name as "inventor" appears on a subsequent edition of 1601. Cort is mainly known for his engravings after other masters; the attribution remains doubtful, though it is attractive, since he is of northern, that is, Dutch, origin.

In fact, the character of this sheet differs from Bruegel's. Here is a meticulous hand, and a soberness unaware of the greater master's fancies. The quiet hamlet, the densely knit front of houses and vegetation, bespeak a sensitive and acute eye, and a synopsis of its own kind. Whoever the "Master of the Small Landscapes" is, he anticipates the domestic landscape of Holland which will come to the fore in the next century.

Hans Bol
Malines 1534–1593 Amsterdam

38. *The Month of March: Planting Vines*
Signed "Hans Bol" and dated 1573
Pen, 172 × 259 mm (6 3/4 × 10 3/16")
British Museum, London, No. 1910.2.12.120

BIBL. : H. G. Franz, "Hans Bol als Landschaftszeichner," *Jahrbuch des Kunsthistorischen Instituts der Universität Graz*, I, 1965, pp. 19 ff, No. 73.

The Four Seasons and the Twelve Months adorned the portals of Gothic cathedrals, and they remained a frequent subject through the eighteenth century—every era giving its own version of work, play, and nature in the cycle of the year.

Bol made several such suites, in drawing and print. One has to forget the grandiose "Months" of Pieter Bruegel to relish Bol's plainspoken narrative. In a quaint mixture of dignity and homeliness, it spins a yarn of weather and land, of trees and vines, of cottages, churches, and castles. The peasants, in their Italianate postures, are almost too stately for their humble labor.

Paul Bril
Antwerp 1554–1626 Rome

39. *A River Plain Between Rocky Mountains, with Noah's Ark*
Inscribed "P. Bril," probably by a later hand
c. 1590
Pen, 195 × 278 mm (7 11/16 × 10 15/16")
Collection F. Lugt, Institut Néerlandais, Paris, No. J. 589

BIBL. : C. van Hasselt and A. Blankert, Exhibition Catalogue, *Artisti Olandesi e Fiamminghi in Italia,* Florence, 1966, No. 16.

Sometimes, an artist attracts us not only for his own sake, but also because his life and work brings a whole era of the past to life for us. We visualize Paul Bril in the Rome of the 1590s, the time when it was built up into a coherent city, and took on the new face that it would keep until the nineteenth century. He got his share in that huge architectural enterprise, obtaining numerous commissions to decorate interiors of palaces and churches with frescoes of landscape.

Landscape had become a branch of its own, one in which Northerners were welcome, and where they made a signal contribution. Bril's large *oeuvre* of drawings bears witness that landscape drawings were also in demand then. They cover a wide range of subjects: Roman topography, marines, woods, mountains, and—in his last year—Italianate forests, already in the "classical" manner.

The example shown is of Bril's middle period, and still reflects Pieter Bruegel. The country gains distinction by taking part in a momentous event: it is the morning after the Deluge, when the Ark has settled on top of Mount Ararat, when the clouds recede before the rising sun, and God the Father sends His rainbow. Fittingly, the earth is empty of its former inhabitants. The solemnity is tempered here with a pleasurable soberness; even with a dash of humor, it seems.

In the opinion of Van Hasselt and Blankert, the sheet is perhaps not in Bril's own hand. Yet it is so typical of his style and, moreover, so ingenious that I cannot resist presenting it here.

Gillis van Coninxloo
Antwerp 1544–1607 Amsterdam

40. *Interior of a Swampy Forest, with a Building in the Distance*
Pen over black chalk, 206×321 mm (8 1/8×12 5/8″)
Royal Museum of Art, Brussels. Collection de Grez, No. 924

BIBL. : Exhibition Catalogue, *Tekeningen . . . uit de Verzameling de Grez,* Museum Boymans-van
Beuningen, Rotterdam, 1954/55, No. 4.
H. Wellensiek, Exhibition Catalogue, *Die Frankenthaler Maler,* Mannheim and Frankenthal,
1962.
H. G. Franz, "De Boslandschappen van Gillis Coninxloo en hun Voorbeeld," *Bulletin
Museum Boymans-van Beuningen,* 1963, pp. 66 ff.
H. G. Franz, *Niederländische Landschaftsmalerei im Zeitalter des Manierismus,* Graz, 1969,
pp. 277 ff.

It will be recalled that German art was partial to trees and forests, but it was Flanders that made them a genre of its own. Gillis van Coninxloo probably knew Titian's woods from prints, but he gave them a deeper shade, and such abundance and density that Max Friedländer speaks of an "orgy of foliage."

The reader will notice that repeatedly in the latter part of the sixteenth century, a master who was born in Flanders died in another country. This was the age of religious strife, when many Flemings who converted to Protestantism had to emigrate, and they spread their art abroad. Coninxloo settled from 1587 to 1595 in the colony of Protestants at Frankenthal, near Frankfort, the home of Adam Elsheimer. His forests made a mark upon the German, who in turn transplanted them later to Italy.

The drawing, perhaps of the Frankenthal period, is unusually summary. It looks like the outline for a painting rather than a finished piece.

Rubens also had a liking for such forests with wild roots, fallen trees, and swamps.

Jacques de Gheyn II
Antwerp 1565–1629 The Hague

41. *Mountains, River, and Sea Under a Stormy Sky;*
    Highway Robbers in the Foreground
    Signed "I Gheyn fc. Anno 1609"
    Pen, brown and gray wash, 171×232 mm (6 3/4×9 1/8″)
    Victoria and Albert Museum, London. Dyce Collection, No. 504

BIBL. : J. Q. van Regteren Altena, *The Drawings of Jacques de Gheyn,* Amsterdam, 1936.

A drawing by De Gheyn goes straight to the connoisseur's heart. It is a joy to follow the line running its curves, rounding and hatching the shapes. With good reason, the pages are highly coveted.

Although the artist's life extends well into the seventeenth century, he still belongs to the sixteenth. His landscapes are in the earlier, "fantastic" manner of his teacher Goltzius, and even outdo it. The earth is molded into massive formations, bare to such a degree that large stretches look as if they were covered with lava. The country appears desolate, almost eerie; robbery and murder fit this mood to a nicety. One remembers that De Gheyn is a contemporary of Shakespeare, and such a landscape could well serve as scenery for *Macbeth* or *King Lear*.

There is a strain of eccentricity in the artist. He is fond of witches, gypsies; he makes a soldier point the gun toward the spectator. Even some of his friendlier subjects, a little mouse, a leaf, are puzzling in their uncanny precision. One feels a measure of genuine greatness and, at the same time, is bewildered by its odd expression.

Jan Brueghel the Elder
Brussels 1568–1625 Antwerp

42. *Seashore with Boats and People, in a Strong Gale*
Signed "Bruegel fecit primo decembri 1614"
Pen with brown and blue washes, 195 × 301 mm (7 11/16 × 11 7/8")
Kupferstichkabinett, Staatliche Museen, West Berlin, No. 724

BIBL. : M. Winner, "Zeichnungen des älteren Jan Brueghel," *Jahrbuch der Berliner Museen*, III, 1961, pp. 190 ff.

It would not be fair to measure Jan Brueghel by the standard of his father Pieter. Jan's art is intimate; his paintings usually are small and richly colored. He was a pupil of Coninxloo, uncommonly hardworking and versatile. Highly successful, he worked for a time for Emperor Rudolph II in Prague, the same ruler who owned so many works of Pieter. Jan also did landscapes and flowers in Rubens' paintings—he was an excellent complement to the younger and greater master.

The early landscape drawings report on his travels in Italy, Germany, and Bohemia. Those of the later years stay within the domestic boundary: country roads with carriages and cattle, villages with travelers, canals with barges and sailors. Mostly done in pen and clear washes, they enchant through their precision and sense of order. This scene by the sea on a gusty day in winter is exceptionally free, and one of his best. A comparison with Pieter's seascape (plate 36) is instructive.

Roelant Savery
Courtrai 1576–1639 Utrecht

43. *Mountainous Country with Rocks, a River, and a Large Building*
Pen in brown and red inks, brown and blue washes, 417×305 mm
(16 3/8 × 12″)
Rijksprentenkabinet, Amsterdam, No. Z.I. 238

BIBL. : Exhibition Catalogue, *Roelandt Savery,* Musée des Beaux-Arts, Ghent, 1954, No. 119.

Like Jan Brueghel, Savery served the Habsburgs for a while, first Rudolph II at Prague, and then Matthias at Vienna. Catering to the encyclopedic appetite of his patrons for scientific curios, he painted and drew exotic animals and flowers, Alpine wildernesses with craggy precipices, giant pine trees.

Savery's landscapes approach the border of the next century. The towering rocks in this drawing, set against the distance, are meant to be spectacular, yet the country as a whole does not strike us as arbitrary. It is rather accommodating, cut to the mileage of a potential traveler. The monastery in the middle ground seems to have a name—perhaps it can be found somewhere in Bohemia or Austria.

The sheet is unusually large, and one of the artist's most ambitious. Lambert Doomer (1624–1700) made a copy after it, increasing the contrast of light and shade, and adding birds and clouds (reproduced in W. Bernt, *Die Niederländischen Zeichner des 17. Jahrhunderts,* Munich, 1957, No. 182).

Federico Zuccaro
Sant' Angelo in Vado 1541/2–1609 Ancona

44. *Pine Forest near Vallombrosa*
Inscribed "1576 adì agosto"
Black and red chalk, 217 × 396 mm (8 1/2 × 15 5/8")
Albertina, Vienna, No. 13329

BIBL. : D. Heikamp, "Federico Zuccaro a Firenze," *Paragone,* No. 205, 1967, pp. 44 ff.
J. Gere, Exhibition Catalogue, *Dessins de Taddeo et Federico Zuccaro,* Louvre, Paris, 1969.

Fittingly, our first choice from the later *Cinquecento* is Federico Zuccaro who then was the chief spokesman of the great Italian tradition and of its *maniera.* By 1575, he had become so renowned that he, a non-Florentine, was commissioned to complete the ceiling frescoes in the Dome which Vasari had left unfinished at his death.

The majority of Federico's drawings are designs for paintings. However, a number of drawings have come down to us which are no more than personal mementos, such as views of Florence and the environs, artists studying the Medici Tombs, or himself in discussion with friends, etc. Here is a pine forest in the mountains near the monastery of Vallombrosa where he spent a summer vacation. He shows himself busily drawing, his sword laid aside, while a companion is picnicking.

Such records, delightfully at variance with Zuccaro's official production, nonetheless reveal the directness and assurance innate in Italian art. The masterly breadth of the page, the proud stance of the trees, hark back to Fra Bartolommeo and Titian. In this forest, the wanderer does not get lost as in Coninxloo's (plate 40).

Black and red chalks are applied alternately, producing an effect quite different from that when used in combination.

Konrad Oberhuber has only recently identified the drawing as a work by Federico Zuccaro.

Giuseppe Cesari, called Il Cavaliere d'Arpino
Arpino 1568–1640 Rome

45. *View of a Town on the Banks of a River*
Black chalk, 281 × 428 mm (11 1/16 × 16 7/8″)
Kupferstichkabinett, Staatliche Museen, West Berlin, No. 15290

A landscape drawing by the Cavaliere d'Arpino is a rarity. I know only two, both in Berlin. They were acquired by the Kupferstichkabinett in 1844, with a large lot of his drawings, from the Pacetti Collection (Lugt 2056a, 2057), which in turn had been assembled in the eighteenth century. Thus their authenticity is assured.* Possibly some more can be discovered in the Uffizi or the Louvre, the two richest depositories of Italian drawings.

Cesari mostly drew figures, in preparation for his commissions of frescoes. Eminently successful, he was active mainly at Rome from 1590 on, at the same time as the Carracci and Caravaggio. In contrast to them, he still clung to the tradition of the Zuccari. The last representative of "Mannerism," he was soon to be considered outmoded and to be superseded by the new style of the *Seicento*.

In this piece, the proud masts, the expressive shapes of the hulls, the postures of the figures betray the artist's fondness for a grandiose manner—here contrasting in an odd, yet very attractive, way with the informality of the subject. The locality has not been identified; we do not even know whether it is the Tiber in Rome.

* Mr. Jacob Bean, Curator of Drawings, The Metropolitan Museum of Art, New York kindly drew my attention to the drawing. I owe the information on its provenance to Dr. Matthias Winner, Director of the Kupferstichkabinett, Berlin.

Girolamo Muziano
Brescia 1532–1592 Rome

46. *Landscape of Mountains and a River*
Pen in brown ink, over black chalk, 490×367 mm (19 1/4×14 7/16")
Uffizi, Florence, No. 522 P

BIBL. : J. C. J. Bierens de Haan, *L'Oeuvre gravé de Cornelis Cort,* The Hague, 1948, pp. 121 ff.
U. Procacci, "Una 'vita' inedita del Muziano," *Arte Veneta,* VIII, 1954, pp. 242 ff.
W. Friedlaender, *Caravaggio Studies,* Princeton, 1955, pp. 64 ff.
A. R. Turner, *The Vision of Landscape in Renaissance Italy,* Princeton, 1966.

Muziano was schooled at Padua (where he met Domenico Campagnola) and at Venice. He moved to Rome in 1549, where he became known for his landscapes as "il giovane de' paesi." A series of seven drawings, all wildernesses with penitent hermits, was engraved by Cornelis Cort in 1573/75. The suite became very popular; in the eighteenth century, it was still considered by Mariette as the most beautiful sequence of landscapes.

This sheet, though not belonging to the series, no doubt was also intended for a print. It documents Muziano's style and historical position well, halfway between Titian and Agostino Carracci. A blessing monk and a crouched woman are only outlined in chalk, but the unfinished state does not diminish the strength of the large drawing.

126

Jacopo Ligozzi
Verona 1547–1626 Florence

47. *Dante in the Dark Forest*
Signed "Iacopo Ligozzi inventor 1587"
Pen, heightened in white with the brush, 200×275 mm (7 7/8 × 10 13/16")
Christ Church, Oxford (Reproduced by permission of the Governing Body
   of Christ Church)

BIBL. : M. Bacci and A. Forlani, *Catalogo di Disegni di Jacopo Ligozzi,* Florence, 1961.
    R. L. McGrath, "Some Drawings by Jacopo Ligozzi Illustrating 'The Divine Comedy'," *Master Drawings,* V, 1967, pp. 31 ff.

Ligozzi joined the court of the Medici about 1575. One of his assignments was to draw the animals and plants which Aldovandri, the Florentine scientist, collected. Over a hundred sheets are preserved in the Uffizi, large-sized like Audubon's, richly colored and scrupulously exact.

Ligozzi called himself "Miniator." The métier of manuscript illumination was even then obsolete, but the technique still is apparent in this drawing. Perhaps there is also a link to the German chiaroscuro tradition.

Dante emerges from the dense forest, just at the hour when the sun is setting (*Inferno,* I, 16–27). The raking light on oaks and figure has an unusual, if somewhat mannered, beauty. This illustration is the best of four (Oxford and Vienna) for the "Divine Comedy"—probably a large project which remained unfinished.

Federico Barocci
Urbino 1526–1612 Urbino

48. *Hills and Trees*
Signed "Federicus Barotius Urbinas fecit"
c. 1575
Brown, gray, green, and red washes over some black chalk; heightened in
  gray and yellow, 393 × 249 mm (15 1/2 × 9 13/16")
British Museum, London, No. P.p. 3–202

BIBL. : H. Olsen, *Federico Barocci,* Copenhagen, 1962, No. 28.

Although Barocci was much older than Ligozzi (plate 47), he appears more advanced, and already seems to anticipate the seventeenth century. The sheet brings to mind the style of Rubens' landscape drawings.

Barocci prepared his finished works extensively, in many studies of bodies, hands, garments—after the model. This landscape, too, may well be based on a study from nature. It is a design for his etching *Stigmatization of Saint Francis* (Bartsch, 3), which Olsen dates about 1575.

Barocci stayed away from the centers of Renaissance art; after two short stages in Rome, he spent his long life in Urbino. His art owes much to Correggio; indeed, this landscape, in its rich coloring, has some of that master's "vaghezza," of his sensuous and hard-to-define intensity.

Agostino Carracci
Bologna 1557–1602 Parma

49. *Mountain Landscape with the Story of the Good Samaritan*
c. 1595/1600
Pen in bister, with slight washes, 273 × 200 mm (10 3/4 × 7 7/8″)
Albertina, Vienna, No. 2121

BIBL. : D. Mahon, Exhibition Catalogue, *Mostra dei Carracci, Disegni,* Bologna, 1956, No. 83.
E. Knab, Exhibition Catalogue, *Claude Lorrain und die Meister der Römischen Landschaft im XVII. Jahrhundert,* Vienna, 1964/65, No. 9.

The brothers Agostino and Annibale Carracci, together with their older cousin Lodovico, founded the "Accademia degli Incamminati" (Academy of the Progressive) in Bologna, in opposition to the prevailing "Mannerism." Of the three, Annibale became the genuine innovator. Agostino is more tradition-bound and less imaginative. His page links up with Venetian landscape, specifically with drawings of Muziano (plate 46); it is their plausible, if freer, continuation.

In this sheet, the hand of a printmaker is recognizable, one who delineates the objects graphically and likes to present a well-filled page. Country and figures do not relate as in the subtle mode of Annibale. Yet the event in the foreground makes an eloquent counterpart to the secluded lake and mountains. In its solidity and deftness, the drawing is impressive.

Annibale Carracci
Bologna 1560–1609 Rome

50. *Landscape with Jacob's Dream*
Inscribed "di mano di Anniballe Carracci" by a later hand
c. 1595
Pen and brush over traces of black chalk, 413 × 262 mm (16 1/4 × 10 5/16″)
The Metropolitan Museum of Art, New York City, No. 19.76.14

BIBL.: P. A. Tomory, *The Ellesmere Collection of Old Master Drawings,* Leicester, 1954.
F. Stampfle and J. Bean, Exhibition Catalogue, *Drawings from New York Collections II, The Seventeenth Century in Italy,* New York, 1967, No. 10.

Annibale Carracci rings in the great era of Italian landscape. He moved to Rome in 1595, which seems to be the approximate time of this drawing. In fact, a similar landscape in the Ellesmere Collection is dated 1595 (Tomory, No. 64).

In the background, a ladder with angels can be spotted, but to make this scene the Dream of Jacob was probably an afterthought, for the whole tenor is rather one of genre. A young person, fallen asleep in the open, unaware of what is around—a poetic motif, favorite long since, has here been invested with a new charm. The youngster not merely is in the landscape, but he helps make it. There is a relation of affinity and contrast between his unconscious presence, the majestic tree, the country behind. The outdoors has become personalized, so to say.

The tree and the rushes hark back to Paul Bril, and the figure still has a Mannerist heaviness, but the mood, in its blend of solemnity and grace, is Annibale's.

Annibale Carracci

51. *Landscape with the Body of Judas*
     c. 1600
     Pen, 229 × 205 mm (9 × 8 1/16″)
     The Louvre, Paris, No. 7436

BIBL. : D. Mahon, Exhibition Catalogue, *Mostra dei Carracci, Disegni,* Bologna, 1956, No. 245.
R. Bacou, Exhibition Catalogue, *Dessins des Carrache,* Paris, 1961, No. 101.

Similar in layout, this landscape is more of one piece than the preceding one and seems to date from the artist's mature period, toward the end of his work at the Galleria Farnese.

The drawing presents the grim story of Judas, who has hanged himself, and the purse of thirty silver pieces on a tree near Golgotha. Jerusalem lies in the distance. Annibale's version deviates somewhat from Matthew 27: 3–5.

Apparently, the page has been cut on both sides, perhaps also on top. If the kneeling man at the left and the cross at the right were complete, the consonance of all parts, of narrative and country, would be even more forceful.

A few years later, in 1603, Annibale painted the Aldobrandini lunettes, the first "classically" built landscapes of the *Seicento*.

Adam Elsheimer

Frankfort 1578–1610 Rome

52. *Wooded Hills Behind a Lake; Shepherds Around a Fire at Night*
Black and white gouache on red-grounded paper, 87×155 mm
(3 7/16×6 1/4″)
The Louvre, Paris, No. 18.658

BIBL. : H. Möhle, *Die Zeichnungen Adam Elsheimers,* Berlin, 1966, No. 46.
J. G. van Gelder and I. Jost, "Elsheimers Unverteilter Nachlass," *Simiolus,* 2, chap. 3 (Zeichnungen), 1967/68, pp. 23 ff.
K. Andrews, Review of Möhle, *Master Drawings,* 6, 1968, pp. 158 ff.

Seicento landscape grew from a confluence of different currents. Various Italian and northern traditions joined together—an international feat that could happen only in Rome. Rome, herself poor in native talents, had the distinction of letting newcomers use their own idiom. Therefore, "ideal" landscape, "classical" landscape are terms which cover many things. The nuance of the individual artist has to be discerned within the common trend.

Germany's contribution was Adam Elsheimer who settled in the city in 1600, and died, prematurely, in 1610. An early influence from the Flemish school in Frankenthal (plate 40) was superseded by that of the Bavarian Hans Rottenhammer, whose assistant he became in Venice in 1598. Indeed, Elsheimer's art is essentially German. Here again is nature talking about herself, communicating her "feeling," but now in the language of the seventeenth century. It is the pervasive aura that speaks to us; it lies over water and trees, blends land and sky, and fills the dusky atmosphere. The chiaroscuro technique underlines the semidarkness. Elsheimer's chiaroscuro is more gentle than that of Caravaggio, who worked in Rome at the same time.

The artist must have considered his landscapes in gouache as finished works, equal to paintings. Möhle lists twenty-two, all on grounded paper, some varicolored. Van Gelder and Jost have questioned the authenticity of the group and ascribed a large part of it to minor, and much later, Dutch masters. The problem remains wide open. This piece, however, is generally accepted; the homogeneity and the attention to detail speak strongly in favor of Elsheimer's authorship.

Adam Elsheimer

53. *Italian Mountains with a Train of Mules*
    Pen, light brown and grayish brown washes, 134×160 mm (5 1/4×6 5/16″);
    a margin of about 25 mm at the top, originally empty, has been filled
    in by a later hand
    Kupferstichkabinett, Staatliche Museen, West Berlin, No. 12333

BIBL. : Möhle, *op. cit.,* No. 26.

The attribution to Elsheimer has been doubted; in my opinion, the fluency of technique and layout, the sureness of the spatial recession agree well with his style.

Möhle dates the drawing 1607/8. Rubens, who had been acquainted with Elsheimer in those years, wrote to a common friend in Rome when he heard of the master's untimely death: "I pray that God will forgive Signor Adam his sin of sloth, by which he has deprived the world of the most beautiful things, [and] caused himself much misery . . ." (R. Magurn, *The Letters of P. P. Rubens,* Cambridge, Mass., 1955, p. 54).

From this sketch, one would not guess that Elsheimer was a slow and inhibited worker. It shows a genuine and immediate comprehension of the country. The spread of the verdant slopes across the page, paralleled by the mule train, expresses summarily what seventeenth-century landscape later will say in explicit terms.

Guido Reni
Calvenzano 1575–1642 Bologna

54. *An Old Town on a Rocky Promontory, Overlooking the Sea*
Pen, 200 × 273 mm (7 7/8 × 10 3/4")
The Louvre, Paris, No. 8927

BIBL. : W. Vitzthum, Review of exhibition "Claude Lorrain und die Meister der Römischen
Landschaft im XVII. Jahrhundert," *Master Drawings*, III, 1965, p. 179.
C. Johnston, "Reni Landscape Drawings in Mariette's Collection," *Burlington Magazine*,
1969, pp. 377 ff.

To those of us who were reared at a time when "Guido Reni's emptiness roused the laughter" (Berenson), the spectacular comeback of the *Seicento* was perplexing. That the reappraisal was first made in sweeping and worn terms like "classicism" or "baroque" added to the difficulty. Since then, research and exhibitions have helped to discern the nuances and to read the individual idioms within the generic style. It is significant that Reni's art recently has been characterized as "ferma contemplazione" by Gnudi, as "classicismo cristiano" and "sostanza puritana" by Emiliani (Exhibition Catalogue, *L'Ideale Classico del Seicento,* Bologna, 1962).

Naturally, from one single drawing, and of a subject unusual with Reni, the master cannot be truly appreciated. Even so, one sees not only a facile hand, but a touch of that genuine nobility which gives distinction to all his work. Furthermore, the "progress" since the Carracci is evident; this is a fully articulated *Seicento* composition.

Domenichino (Domenico Zampieri)
Bologna 1581–1641 Naples

55. *A Mountainous Landscape with a Monastery*
1620/25
Red chalk, 227×334 mm (8 15/16×13 1/4″)
Museum of Fine Arts, Budapest, No. 1697

BIBL. : J. Pope-Hennessy, *The Drawings of Domenichino . . . at Windsor Castle,* London, 1948.
T. Mullaly, "Domenichino and the New Landscape," *Apollo,* No. 66, August, 1957,
pp. 8 ff.
Exhibition Catalogue, *Meisterzeichnungen aus dem Museum der Schönen Künste in Budapest,*
Graphische Sammlung Albertina, Vienna, 1967, No. 28.

Domenichino, another Bolognese, joined the Carracci to assist on the ceiling frescoes of the Farnese Gallery, and later became one of the most sought-after artists in Rome. His paintings of landscape carry on Annibale's style; they are less subtle, but more strongly articulated and studiously organized. Poussin must have taken a good look at his work.

One wonders whether this monastery, seated majestically above lake and trees, represents a factual locality. To accentuate a landscape by a large rock or building in the center is a device frequently used by Domenichino. He sometimes did draw after the motif, but then in ink and in a less elaborate manner.

Guercino (Giovanni Francesco Barbieri)
Cento 1591–1666 Bologna

56. *A Fortified Town on a Hill*
Pen in bister, 286 × 213 mm (11 1/4 × 8 3/8″)
Royal Library, Windsor Castle, No. 2762 (Reproduced by gracious permission of Her Majesty the Queen)

BIBL. : D. Mahon, Exhibition Catalogue, *Il Guercino, Disegni,* Bologna, 1968, No. 204.

To reach for the quill and brush must have come as naturally as breathing to Guercino. His drawings in public and private collections probably run into the thousands; even in the lean market of today, a sheet by Guercino turns up frequently. His favorite mediums were pen and bister, and sanguine. Many imitations also exist, not always easy to spot. The drawings at Windsor are endorsed by an excellent provenance; George III acquired them directly from the descendants of the artist.

After having trained one's eye in looking through many Guercino drawings, one believes that a genuine work can also be recognized by stylistic evidence. Guercino's hand has a superb freedom and sureness. There is nothing vague nor mechanical. However hasty the outlines or washes, they clearly define the shapes and the spatial relations. His pages have a distinctive radiance which bespeaks the splendor of all created things. The rise of this imaginary southern town from the shore, the colorful bustle, strike a genial, lyrical, and most endearing note.

Bartholomeus Breenbergh

Deventer 1598/1600–1657 Amsterdam

57. *View in the Gardens of Castello Bomarzo, near Viterbo*
Inscribed "A Castel Bomarso"; signed "B Breenbergh f. a Roma 1625"
Pen and brush in bister and Chinese ink, 410×280 mm (16 1/4×11")
Collection F. Lugt, Institut Néerlandais, Paris, No. J.4478 verso

BIBL. : E. Knab, "Die Anfänge des Claude Lorrain," *Jahrbuch der Kunsthistorischen Sammlungen in Wien,* 1960, pp. 63 ff.
Exhibition Catalogue, *Nederlandse 17e Eeuwse Italianiserende Landschapschilders,* Utrecht, 1965, No. 25.
C. van Hasselt, Exhibition Catalogue, *Dessins de Paysagistes Hollandais du XVIIe Siècle de la Collection Particulière conservée à l'Institut Néerlandais de Paris,* 1968/69, No. 24.
M. Roethlisberger, *Bartholomäus Breenbergh, Handzeichnungen,* Berlin, 1969, No. 43.

Here is one of the spots which Breenbergh drew in and around Rome. The young Dutchman had come to the city in 1619, and readily assimilated the example which Bril, Elsheimer, and Poelenburgh had set, with a fresh eye. The washes of this sheet suggest the southern light with a skill that anticipates Claude Lorrain. It can even be assumed that such drawings—dated between 1625 and 1627—had an influence upon Claude, whose independent career started about 1630.

To measure Breenbergh against the great Frenchman would be unfair, of course. He can be appreciated by his own standard. He has the Netherlandish touch; sunlight and shadows lie deftly upon the ground and bring forth the specific formation and luminosity of this hillside.

At about the same time, Breenbergh's colleagues in the North discovered the "Dutchness" of Holland. Breenbergh's aim is the same, only the topography is different.

The landscape on the recto has been used by the artist for several paintings.

Nicolas Poussin
Les Andelys 1594–1665 Rome

58. *The Aventine Hill in Rome*
c. 1642
Bister wash over black chalk, 134×312 mm (5 1/4×12 1/4″)
Uffizi, Florence, No. 8101 recto

BIBL. : W. Friedlaender and A. Blunt, *The Drawings of Nicolas Poussin,* London, 1963, Vol. IV, No. 277.

Among Poussin's drawings there are about a dozen landscapes, some after nature, like this view of the Aventine Hill seen from the Ripa Grande across the Tiber. Hill and buildings have not changed much since then.

Reni or Guercino would have looked at Rome with a different eye. Here is the eminent Frenchman's attitude, austere and pointed; at the same time, perceptive of the precious surfaces and of the figuration of light and shadow. One follows the horizontal riverbank, the diagonal path bordered with trees, then back along the buildings—a scaffolding of singular strength.

The sun stands behind the trees, the hour is before noon. One is aware of time also in a more relevant sense: this is an hour of Rome, one hour in its vast existence. The historical situation, essential in all Poussin's creation, gives distinction to this drawing.

Nicolas Poussin

59. *A Sunny Plain with an Arch; Hills in the Distance*
1640 or 1642
Bister wash, with some pen, over black chalk, 219 × 277 mm (8 5/8 × 10 7/8")
Musée Condé, Chantilly, No. P 198

BIBL. : W. Friedlaender and A. Blunt, *op. cit.,* No. 272.
R. Bacou, Exhibition Catalogue, *Le Cabinet d'un grand amateur, P.-J. Mariette,* Paris, 1967,
p. 154.

The context of time is intrinsic to this landscape, one of Poussin's most grandiose. The vast plain lies under an intense light, and like the Aventine Hill, is filled with a pregnant atmosphere.

It has always been taken for granted that it shows the Campagna with a Roman arch. However, Roseline Bacou has recently identified the locality as Villeneuve-lès-Avignon, with the Fort Saint-André, seen across the Rhône from Avignon. This surprising discovery gives the choice between two dates: either November 1640 when Poussin probably traveled through Avignon, on the way to Paris; or October 1642 when, as we know for sure, he did so on returning to Rome. The later date appears more likely.

Claude Gellée, called Le Lorrain
Chamagne 1600–1682 Rome

60. *View of Saint Peter's in Rome, from the Pamphili Garden*
Inscribed "A M. De Bertaine faict par moi/Claude Gellee dit il lorains. a
Roma/ce 22 maigio 1646. la vuie de la/vigne du papa innocent et st.
piere de Roma 1647"
Pen and brush in bister, some black chalk and gouache, 212×314 mm
(8 5/16×12 3/8")
British Museum, London, No. 067–151

BIBL. : M. Roethlisberger, *Claude Lorrain, The Drawings,* Berkeley and Los Angeles, Cal., 1968,
No. 619.

Claude was born in Lorraine, which means, within the orbit of French language and civilization. Like scores of artists from Italy and all Europe, he was drawn to Rome, then bustling with building and decorating, where an aspiring young man could expect employment and patronage. He settled in the metropolis about 1626, and soon found the calling for which he was gifted. He did well for himself and never left his adopted country.

At that time, Rome was not nearly as packed as it is today. There were many empty spaces, gardens, and rural plots. The Forum still was the Campo Vaccino, a field for cattle. The herd of goats, grazing near Saint Peter's in this drawing, may well have been on the spot.

It is a strange sensation to look upon the big cupola through Claude's eyes. We know it so well, yet here it somehow appears curiously remote, and seems to have a closer affinity to the far hills and to the orb of the sky than to the topography of the city.

The drawing is a finished product, not preparatory to a painting. The inscription, in the master's usual mixture of French and Italian, indicates locality, date, and the recipient, "Monsieur de Bertaine." The name does not recur elsewhere in Claude's notations.

See also Introduction, p. 23.

Claude Gellée

61. *Mountainous Country near Rome, with Larches and Buildings*
Signed "Claudio fecit"
1638/39
Pen in bister, red and gray washes, 320×222 mm (12 5/8×8 3/4″)
British Museum, London, No. 007–230

BIBL. : M. Roethlisberger, *op. cit.,* No. 395.

Essentially, the theme of Claude Lorrain is ever the same but is modulated in endless variations; equally diverse is his drawing technique. When looking through the hundreds of his drawings in the British Museum, one meets all kinds of mediums: black, gray, and red chalks, bister, and inks of different colors and dilutions; often in combinations that give the page the complexion of a painting. Our selection concentrates on pages where the pen is dominant—easier to reproduce—but it is the brush which brings forth the full warmth and sonority that fill the master's world.

Here, the dark larches and solemn towers strike an unusually grave note. On the verso are several sketches of the port of Civitavecchia. According to Roethlisberger, this makes 1640 the latest possible date for the drawing.

Claude Gellée

62. *A Brook and Trees, with Figures and a Horse*
Signed "Claudio/Cresencia/Roma 1662"
Pen and wash, 183 × 251 mm (7 3/16 × 9 7/8")
British Museum, London, No. 008–242

BIBL. : M. Roethlisberger, *op. cit.,* No. 868.

Joachim von Sandrart, who had lived in Rome until 1635, relates in the *Teutsche Academie* how his friend Claude used to explore the environs of the city and to sketch after nature. Still as an elderly man, Claude occasionally took his drawing tools and set out through one of the Roman gates. After crossing Ponte Molle, he would be in the region of Casale della Crescenza, where he once chanced upon this delightful scene.

However, the drawing clearly speaks about more than a factual observation. The oak and birch bordering the little stream, the people taking their leisure in the shade, the sunny expanse behind—these impart a message of restfulness and contentment, of the concord between nature and man. The theme of European landscape—"How do the two realms fit together?"—here seems to have found the most felicitous and valid answer. This bit of country tells of the generosity of nature; one recognizes that the earth is man's hospitable and perpetual homestead.

See also Introduction

Claude Gellée

63. *A Hill and Trees Above the Tiber Valley,
   in the Distance Mount Soracte*
   1660/65
   Black chalk, pen and brush in bister, 166 × 243 mm (6 1/2 × 9 9/16″)
   British Museum, London, No. 006–118

BIBL. : M. Roethlisberger, *op. cit.,* No. 911.

Claude devised some of his paintings with preliminary sketches, but most of the drawings were ends in themselves. He drew for pleasure and liked to keep his products. In the inventory made after his death, twelve bound volumes are listed (besides the *Liber Veritatis;* plate 65), each containing up to eighty sheets (Roethlisberger, pp. 55 ff.).

In combining black chalk with warm brown bister, the artist achieves here a colorful effect, almost like that of a painting. The very simplicity of the layout accounts for the perfection of the page. We recognize the skyline of Mount Soracte in the distance, but the name is irrelevant in the "fabric of this vision," as it is in Prospero's. Nor is it likely that Claude depicted the site in front of the motif. What he wished to bring forth, the "Stimmung" of Roman landscape, was fully present in his mind. "Stimmung" does not mean a vague mood. Everything has its exact pitch, the parts are tuned to each other with a crystalline precision. One gauges the distances, the height of the birds, the level of the foreground above the valley.

Claude also knows a further dimension: time. The landscape emerges from the vast background of its history, against which the present hour stands out, and from which it derives importance. Space and time are merely two facets of a single aspect. The "here and now" constitutes the personality and identity of the landscape.

See also Introduction, p. 23.

Claude Gellée

64. *Landscape with the Baptism of the Eunuch* (Acts 8: 26–39)
Signed "Claudoi IVF/Romae 1677" (or 1678)
Pen and brush in bister, 227 × 378 mm (8 15/16 × 14 7/8")
British Museum, London, No. 007–147

BIBL. : M. Roethlisberger, *op. cit.,* No. 1106.

More than the other examples, this drawing shows that Claude's landscapes ought not to be viewed from the front. The beholder will take his stand in the middle of the plain, look all around and up to the sky which vaults over the earth like an immense cupola.

The sheet is the design for a painting of 1678 for Cardinal Spada. The composition therefore is more studied, the proportions carefully measured. The story in the center of the stage does not appear significant—though it was so to the Cardinal—except that the small figures emphasize the magnitude of the country. Yet the event strikes a specific note. It is not a mere addition, but on the contrary, the focus of actuality on which the entire country converges.

Roethlisberger suggests an alternate interpretation of the subject: Aeneas and the Cumaean Sibyl (Vergil, *Aeneid,* Book VI). I have no doubt that the traditional title is correct.

See also Introduction, p. 24.

Claude Gellée

65. *View of the Campagna from Tivoli*
c. 1645
Pen and brush in bister, heightened in white, on blue paper, 195 × 262 mm
(7 5/8 × 10 5/16″)
British Museum, London (Chatsworth Settlement, *Liber Veritatis* No. 89)

BIBL. : M. Kitson and M. Roethlisberger, "Claude Lorrain and the *Liber Veritatis*," *Burlington Magazine,* 1959, pp. 14 ff., 328 ff., 381 ff.
M. Roethlisberger, *op. cit.,* No. 573; on *Liber Veritatis,* pp. 63 ff.

Here, the use of drawing is quite special. The page is from the *Liber Veritatis,* a book of copies which Claude himself made *after* his own paintings. Allegedly, he did this to protect himself against imitators—a futile attempt in those times. Perhaps the *Liber Veritatis* served as a sample collection for customers, or, more likely, as a memento which the master wished to keep of his output.

However this may be, it is a rare experience to look through the volume of two hundred drawings and to follow a development of almost fifty years. The style changes slowly. Claude was not given to radical innovations; he even repeated a felicitous composition in a later work. Almost imperceptibly, his art ripens into the great images of his old age.

Our sheet is of the middle period, from about the same time as the view of Saint Peter's. It records a painting now in the British Royal Collection. This was Claude's last topographical picture; afterwards all his landscapes were imaginary.

Naturally, the designs of the *Liber Veritatis* are not as spontaneous as the free drawings. While this view gives an eyeful of the famous site, it does not convey the atmosphere of the painting, Claude's "most spectacular sunset" (Roethlisberger).

Gaspard Dughet
Rome 1615–1675 Rome

66. *Landscape with Elijah and the Angel on Mount Horeb*
(I Kings 19: 11)
Black chalk, heightened in white, 600 × 426 mm (23 5/8 × 16 3/4")
Kunstmuseum, Düsseldorf, No. FP 4740

BIBL. : F. Arcangeli, in Exhibition Catalogue, *L'Ideale Classico del Seicento* . . . , Bologna, 1962, pp. 256 ff., and No. 226.
W. Friedlaender and A. Blunt, *op. cit.,* Vol. IV, pp. 36 ff.
M. R. Waddingham, "The Dughet Problem," *Paragone,* No. 161, 1963, pp. 37 ff.
D. Graf, Exhibition Catalogue, *Meisterzeichnungen der Sammlung Lambert Krahe,* Kunstmuseum, Düsseldorf, 1969/70, No. 114.

Next to Claude Lorrain, Dughet is *the* landscapist of the *Seicento*. His prestige was uneven: very high in Italy and England, where his landscapes passed for the "classical" par excellence; less eminent in France. A French critic remarked: "Il est beau, mais il a deux méchants voisins" (he is beautiful, but has two nasty neighbors). No doubt, Dughet loses out as soon as he is compared to Poussin or Claude. The comparison is not fair, but seems unavoidable.

Gaspard was Poussin's brother-in-law and his pupil in the 1630s. He even assumed his teacher's name and called himself Gaspard Poussin. He was also much indebted to Claude. Is his art then a mere synthesis of the two great Frenchmen?

I believe that he comes into his own if one realizes that he thinks in Italian terms—less subtle, more affirmative than the French. His work does not have Poussin's intellectual transparency, he is unaware of historical and cultural implications, but he has a genuine feeling for the grandeur and the pathos of nature, for the rugged and luxuriant beauty of the Sabine mountains. To a measure, Dughet is the Ruisdael of the South. That he was a passionate huntsman conforms well with his art. The "great and strong wind" which rages over Mount Horeb and fells a tree was familiar to him. Among the drawings, many attributions are still controversial. This sheet is a design for a painting in the National Gallery, London. It belongs to a group of very large dimensions done in chalk, which is generally accepted, and seems to date from his late years. Our example illustrates his majestic and emphatic manner, and his skill in composing a page.

Pier Francesco Mola
Coldrerio 1612–1666 Rome

67. *Mountainous Landscape with an Apple Tree*
Signed "Mola F"
1641
Pen and brush in bister, 285 × 205 mm (11 1/4 × 8 1/16")
British Museum, London, No. 1898.12.16.1

BIBL. : K. T. Parker, *Old Master Drawings,* II, 1927, pp. 23 ff.
J. Rowlands, "Mola's Preparatory Drawings and Some Additions to His *Oeuvre*," *Master Drawings,* II, 1964, pp. 271 ff.

As the seventeenth century advanced in Italy, an expertness in style and technique was attained by which masters beneath the highest rank also could turn out works of remarkable quality. The same is true of Holland about 1650.

This drawing reveals influences from Guercino and Poussin, but assimilated to conform to Mola's own diction. Not often was a page done with such grace and skill.

These are the mountains north of Lake Como, near Coldrerio, where Mola worked in 1641 (a sketch for his fresco in the church is on the verso). The portrayal of actual sites was uncommon in Italy at that time; Mola evidently wished to keep a souvenir of his birthplace. He noted on the sheet "Monte di Samaia Colle di Brusada," "Chiesa di S. Antonio genestre," and, along the tree trunk, "Pianta vechia da Mela nel $\overline{\text{me}}$ Ciosco" (old apple tree at the foot of Mount Ciosco).

Two more views of Coldrerio are in the British Museum; in one of them, camels(!) with their drivers walk up the Alpine road.

Pietro Testa
Lucca 1611–1650 Rome

68. *Mountains, River, and Trees*
Pen and brush, in different shades of bister, 220 × 272 mm (8 5/8 × 10 3/4″)
The Louvre, Paris, No. 1915

BIBL. : A. Marabottini, "Novità sul Lucchesino," *Commentari,* V, 1954, pp. 116 ff., 217 ff.

The style of Pietro Testa is more linear than Mola's. The elongated conduct of his pen anticipates the handwriting of the Tiepolos. This page, in its masterful layout, washed in different shades, is one of his best.

Testa, a pupil of Domenichino, belonged to the circle of Cassiano del Pozzo, the humanist who was Poussin's patron. Contemporary sources describe his fondness for secluded places and his melancholy temperament. His career in Rome was not successful, and his life ended prematurely.

Salvator Rosa
Naples 1615–1673 Rome

69. *The Interior of a Forest with a Youth Reading*
Pen in bister, 296×411 mm (11 5/8×16 3/16″)
Uffizi, Florence, No. 6573 S

BIBL. : L. Salerno, *Salvator Rosa*, Florence, 1963.

Salvator Rosa was a bird of quite another feather from Testa: Neapolitan, extrovert, boastful of his talents as painter, etcher, writer, actor, musician; and ever set against the ruling patrons and fashionable artists. He worked in Florence from 1640 to 1649, and then settled in Rome.

In eighteenth century England, "Salvatore" was famed as one of the three great landscapists (Claude Lorrain and Gaspard Dughet being the others), and as the paragon of the "sublime"—which meant lonely and unhampered nature. To the modern viewer, his landscape paintings are less heart-stirring, and some appear repetitious, perhaps also because many imitations travel under his name. But they indeed initiated a new type, and created a fashion in British paintings and parks. They still were influential with the Romantics of the nineteenth century.

His drawings have a strong appeal. The rough yet powerful handwriting of this page fits the equally unkempt wilderness to which the solitary youth adds his accent.

Stains of oil have impaired the sheet, as often happened in workshops.

Jacques Callot
Nancy 1592–1635 Nancy

70. *A Village Square*
Bister wash over black chalk, 171 × 337 mm (6 3/4 × 13 1/4″)
National Museum, Stockholm, No. 3282/1863

BIBL. : D. Ternois, *Jacques Callot; catalogue complet de son oeuvre dessiné*, Paris, 1962, No. 1338.

Florence produced its own brand of landscape, one different from the Roman. Not much research has been done about it, as the artists are mostly of minor caliber: Poccetti, Parigi, Cantagallina, Bazzicaluva. Yet it is a distinctive tradition, although it manifests itself more in engraving and etching than in painting. The style is linear, the subjects are picturesque and—in decided contrast to Rome—rather low-brow. People in their menial occupations appear in these landscapes which are realistic and often shabby.

Perhaps it was coincidence that Callot spent only a few years in Rome, but about ten in Florence (1612–21). Anyway, he was more receptive to the non-Roman style; conversely, he had a strong impact upon Florentine landscape.

It goes without saying that Callot is a more important artist than those mentioned. This drawing dates many years later, after his return to Nancy. It is hard to decide whether it belongs to the southern or the northern tradition. It certainly is very French. In its wit and conciseness, it forecasts the *dixhuitième*. The sheet is almost entirely done with the brush, a technique also used frequently by Poussin.

174

Stefano della Bella
Florence 1610–1664 Florence

71. *An Italian (or French?) Hamlet in the Mountains*
Pen and brush over some black chalk, 149 × 211 mm (5 7/8 × 8 1/4″)
British Museum, London, No. 1872.10.12.3275

BIBL. : A. Blunt, *The Drawings of G. B. Castiglione and Stefano della Bella . . . at Windsor Castle,* London, 1954.

Stefano della Bella was a prolific draftsman and etcher, strongly influenced by Callot's style. His etchings—over a thousand—cover a large variety of subjects: festivals, decorations, suites of seasons, of *danses macabres,* etc. They are clever and inventive, and were exploited by many artists in the seventeenth and eighteenth centuries.

Stefano lived in Paris for ten years, he traveled to Holland, and his style and motifs attest his acquaintance with northern art.

The prickly penmanship of the drawing, and the subject matter as well, reflect Callot. The village in the mountains is seen from a worm's-eye angle—literally so—and emphasis is laid on its isolation and squalor. The page gains at closer study. It is laid out in the lofty Italian manner, it has some of Guercino's brilliance, and the artist impresses us as a natural and resourceful storyteller. Quite rightly, Blunt points out that Stefano della Bella "ranks high among the petits maîtres."

The drawing may be connected with an etching (A. de Vesme, *Le Peintre-Graveur Italien,* Milan, 1906, No. 825).

Peter Paul Rubens
Siegen 1577–1640 Antwerp

72. *Two Trees*
1617/19
Pen over black chalk, 582×489 mm (22 3/4×19 1/4″)
The Louvre, Paris, No. 20.212

BIBL. : J. Held, *Rubens Selected Drawings,* London, 1959, No. 131.
        H. G. Evers, "Zu einem Blatt mit Zeichnungen von Rubens im Berliner Kupferstich-
        kabinett," *Pantheon,* 19, 1961, pp. 93 ff., 136 ff.

Rubens turned to landscape rather late, about 1618, in the years when he painted hunting scenes. While he did the "Hunts" for his princely patrons, he painted landscapes for his own pleasure and seems to have kept many of them for himself. Yet the mountains and rolling fields, the groves, ponds, and herds, the sunsets, moonlights, and storms bespeak his genius no less than his official production—to some of us even more endearingly.

Only a handful of landscape drawings have been preserved, none with an extensive vista. They show bits of nature, trees, hedges, a part of a meadow. Most are large in scale, much bigger than they look from the reproductions. In the master's words, "the large size of a picture gives one much more courage to express one's ideas clearly and realistically" (R. Magurn, *The Letters of P. P. Rubens,* Cambridge, Mass., 1955, p. 77).

The trees of this drawing—one dead, one alive—are used in the painting of the *Boarhunt* (Dresden), at the core of action, as the spot where the quarry has been brought to bay. When Rubens saw the trees in the fields, was he already looking for such a center, or did it only then occur to him what an exciting game could be built around them? We shall never know. We do know, however, that he set great store by the pathetic motif. He drew the fallen tree a second time lengthwise (Chatsworth) and placed it, several years later, in the *Landscape with Ulysses and Nausicaa* (Pitti, Florence).

Peter Paul Rubens

73. *A Lane in the Woods*
1635/38
Black, red, and white chalk, 383 × 499 mm (15 1/16 × 19 5/8″)
Ashmolean Museum, Oxford, No. 201

BIBL. : J. Held, *op. cit.,* No. 137.

As a rule, the question "real or imaginary?" is beside the point, but Rubens' landscape studies, all directly after the natural motif, tempt us to look over his shoulder and to observe how his eye and mind cooperate, how he transmutes observation into image.

When Rubens sketched the two trees of the preceding drawing, he also encompassed their entire existence. To grow, to stand in the country, to give shade and protection, to die—all this, and more is conveyed. He designs not merely the single specimen, he shows the idea in the particular case, and stores it in his memory (and the page in the portfolio).

This sheet from a later period does more than describe a piece of land: it conveys Nature at work. It is undramatic, and dwells less on particulars than on the whole—the generosity and spaciousness of the earth, the fullness of vegetation, the shimmer of air and foliage.

The woodlands may be those near Steen, the country seat which Rubens had bought in 1635, and where he spent his summers.

Anthony van Dyck
Antwerp 1599-1641 London

74. *A Wooded Hill, with a Farmhouse in the Background*
Signed "A. van Dyck F. 1634"
Pen, 185 × 280 mm (7 1/4 × 11″)
British Museum, London, No. 009-49

BIBL. : H. Vey, *Die Zeichnungen Anton van Dycks,* Brussels, 1962, No. 294.

In his later years, Van Dyck had little time for anything but portraits. Landscape he never painted, but a number of drawings document his liking and skill for it. Stylistically, this sheet belongs to a group of views made in and around Rye in 1633 and 1634, but it probably was done on the Continent: the trees are in full foliage, and Van Dyck left England in March 1634. The stunted growth of oaks, in chalky soil, points to a location close to the sea.

No artist near Rubens could escape the great master's influence, but Van Dyck's hand is clearly different. If the page were unsigned, where would we place it? Venetian landscapes come to mind, but such stylishness and cohesion did not exist at the time of Campagnola. Is it nearer to Reni or Guercino? More attention is given here to detail. Perhaps an astute expert would recognize the Flemish parentage and a similarity to Jan Brueghel.

van dyck F: 1634

Anthony van Dyck

75. *Hills with Meadows, Woods, and a Tower*
Pen; gray, blue, and green watercolor, 228×330 mm (8 15/16×13″)
Collection Duke of Devonshire, Chatsworth, No. 1003 (Reproduced by
permission of the Trustees of the Chatsworth Settlement)

BIBL. : H. Vey, *op. cit.*, No. 306.

The few landscapes with watercolor date from Van Dyck's last years and must represent sites in England. No reproduction can render the delicate and precise nuances of the cool tints.

These are segments of landscape, similar to the backgrounds of portraits; emblems of nature rather than descriptions. They document the master's subtlety and strength, and a superb gift for succinct formulation that shows also in the colors of the paintings, in the features and postures of his sitters. Somehow, Van Dyck seems to forecast the eighteenth century. It is understandable that he set an example for European portraiture, and that his style was determinant in English art for a long time.

Lucas van Uden
Antwerp 1595–1673 Antwerp

76. *Forest Border of Beeches, in a Hilly Country*
Pen, gray and blue washes, 177×208 mm (6 15/16×8 3/16″)
Collection John Witt, London

BIBL. : Y. Thiéry, *Le Paysage Flamand au XVIIe siècle,* Paris-Brussels, 1953, pp. 62 ff.

Lucas van Uden continues the Flemish tradition of Joos de Momper and Jan Brueghel, but enhanced by the model of Rubens. He specialized in landscape; many backgrounds in paintings of Rubens, between the years 1615 and 1630, are supposed to be by his hand.

Compared to the greater master, Van Uden's scope is limited. He pictures the local character of his native land, of the country near Antwerp, hilly or flat, interspersed with castles and windmills, animated by rows of trees; he brings forth its "tender majesty" (Thiéry).

He was a prolific and gifted draftsman, and liked to combine pen with watercolors, delicately blending warm and cool tints. A comparison with a drawing by Vroom (plate 82), similar in subject and technique, shows how far the Dutch and Fleming have moved apart.

Hendrik Goltzius
Venlo 1558–1617 Haarlem

77. *Plain and Dunes near Haarlem*

Inscription "L.V.V." added by a later hand
c. 1603
Pen, 160×286 mm (6 5/16×11 1/4")
Museum Boymans-van Beuningen, Rotterdam, No. DN 199/96

BIBL. : E. K. J. Reznicek, *Die Zeichnungen von Hendrick Goltzius,* Utrecht, 1961, No. 405.

Freely adopting and transmitting styles and trends, Goltzius had a considerable influence on Dutch art of his time. His sizable graphic *oeuvre* is uncommonly versatile in subjects and technique.

The drawings of landscape, about twenty only, fall into two distinct groups. Those of the 1590s depict the rocks, ravines, and waterfalls of Titianesque ancestry, but at the turn of the century, the country changes. The horizon drops to the slight elevation of dunes; we find ourselves amidst the quiet fields near Haarlem.

These "firsts" of Dutch local scenery have a peculiar charm. The delicate pen strokes weave a uniform texture of ground and air, the landscape seems to consist of evenly dispersed matter.

What accounts for the sudden turnabout? Perhaps Goltzius, with his flair for new trends, recognized that the fantastic and exotic manner had to yield to the sober and domestic. He probably knew drawings of Pieter Bruegel (plate 35) and of the Master of the Small Landscapes (plate 37) which showed him the way to a new type of landscape. In fact, it is their technique which he continues. His style is that of the sixteenth century, quite different from the wiry lines and angular forms used by the pioneers of the next generation, Buytewech, Visscher, and Esaias van de Velde.

In his excellent monograph, Reznicek describes the historical place of Goltzius' landscape, its antecedents, its relation to his contemporaries, and its later influence (pp. 177–84).

Esaias van de Velde
Amsterdam 1590/91–1630 The Hague

78. *Village at the Border of a Canal*
Inscribed "EVV" by a later hand
Pen and wash, 185 × 291 mm (7 1/4 × 11 7/16")
Rijksprentenkabinet, Amsterdam, No. 9660

BIBL. : W. Stechow, "Esaias van de Velde and the Beginnings of Dutch Landscape Painting,"
Nederlands Kunsthistorisch Jaarboek, I, 1947.
K. G. Boon and L. C. J. Frerichs, Exhibition Catalogue, *Dessins Hollandais du Siècle d'Or,*
Brussels, 1961, No. 30.
W. Stechow, *Dutch Landscape Painting of the Seventeenth Century,* London, 1966.

Esaias van de Velde is a key figure in the early part of Holland's "golden age." He settled in Haarlem in 1610, perhaps attracted by Goltzius. A glance back to Hans Bol (plate 38) shows how much landscape has changed since the previous century, from a voluble narrative of country and people to this concise and restrained statement. It strikes one almost like an exercise in a new discipline.

The drawing leaves much unsaid; it makes us guess rather than see. Yet it conveys, in a nutshell, the character of the small hamlet under the elms, and its modest living circle—although no people are visible. In Stechow's words: "a" Dutch landscape, not a topographical record.

In the work of Esaias, nature is meager, and presents herself in her winter, rather than in her summer, dress.

190

Claes Jansz. Visscher
Amsterdam 1587–1652 Amsterdam

79. *Haarlem with the River Spaarne*
1610/20
Pen, brown and blue washes, 184×308 mm (7 1/4×12 1/8″)
Museum Boymans-van Beuningen, Rotterdam, No. 1952/T. 10

BIBL. : E. Haverkamp Begemann, *Bulletin Museum Boymans,* April 1952, p. 72.
W. Stechow, *op. cit.,* p. 18.

Visscher, a pupil of Jacques de Gheyn (plate 41), became an engraver and publisher of portraits, maps, and topographical views, after his own and other artists' designs.

The scrupulous and clear-cut lines show the hand of the printmaker; beyond that, the drawing bespeaks the new spirit of Dutch landscape. The view of Haarlem, while recording the city and its river, also suggests the unruffled mood of the day, and the life running its course under the large sky. Here is not yet the animation which will pervade Dutch landscapes twenty years later; the tone is still muted, but it sounds in a distinct voice.

Willem Buytewech
Rotterdam 1591–1624 Rotterdam

80. *A Ruined Castle Among Trees*
Signed "WB"
After 1617
Pen, 144×350 mm (5 11/16×13 3/4")
Collection F. Lugt, Institut Néerlandais, Paris, No. 2356

BIBL. : E. Haverkamp Begemann, *Willem Buytewech,* Amsterdam, 1959, No. 110.
     C. van Hasselt, Exhibition Catalogue, *Dessins de Paysagistes Hollandais du XVIIe siècle . . . ,*
        1968/69, No. 27.

Buytewech's nickname, "geestige Willem"—sharp-witted Bill—fits the drawing nicely. There is a keen mind in the angular structure and the over-precise texture (note the chestnut tree next to the tower). The landscape is stylish to such a degree that it looks curiously detached, even remote, and makes us wonder what is behind those walls and trees.

It is true that Dutch art, from Goltzius to Van Goyen, brings nature closer to the beholder, but a work like this one cautions against generalizations. It portends a different, almost opposite trend, one which finds its grandest expression in the paintings and etchings of Hercules Seghers.

In the year 1612, Buytewech, with Esaias van de Velde and Seghers, joined the guild of Saint Luke in Haarlem, then a center of art, and especially prominent in landscape.

Hercules Seghers
Haarlem c. 1590–before 1638 The Hague

81. *A Farmhouse Under Trees, a Man Seated on a Railing*
c. 1620
Yellow and gray washes over black chalk, on gray-grounded paper,
176×291 mm (6 7/8×11 1/2″)
Rijksprentenkabinet, Amsterdam

BIBL. : J. Springer, *Die Radierungen des Hercules Seghers,* Berlin, 1910/12.
W. Stechow, *op. cit.*
K. G. Boon, Exhibition Catalogue, *Hercules Seghers,* Amsterdam, 1967, No. T. 1.

Through his apprenticeship in Amsterdam under Coninxloo, Seghers is linked to the tradition of Bruegel. Then, as master in Haarlem, he strove for a new kind of landscape, as did Goltzius, Esaias van de Velde, Visscher, and Buytewech. But it was he who took the decisive step, some time between 1615 and 1620, and found the inner unity of landscape unknown to the preceding century, namely a common denominator for the multitude and diversity of things.

The reader does not expect that the significance of Seghers can be discussed in a few lines about one example. Yet he will not fail to perceive that there is a suspense in the drawing which is absent in Goltzius' landscape (plate 77), that the stillness which reigns between the seated man, the house, and the trees has a different pitch from the quietness in the hamlet of Van de Velde (plate 78). He also will sense duration in the immobility, and will hear the resonance of a vast space.

Seghers is a "primitive" of the new reality, which will be fully articulated by the next generation. He also must have been an uncommonly single-minded person, absorbed by his one idea to the exclusion of all else. Therefore, his landscapes have that hermetic and puzzling character.

The great master can best be studied in his etchings, especially in those with large vistas of Alpine rocks and plateaus. Virtually no drawings exist. This one is authenticated by its provenance and the connection with a print (Springer, 42).

Cornelis Hendriksz. Vroom
Haarlem c. 1591–1661 Haarlem

82. *The River Spaarne at Haarlem*
1625/35
Pen, color washes, 178×312 mm (7×12 1/4″)
British Museum, London, No. 1836.8.11.563

BIBL. : J. Rosenberg, "Cornelis Hendricksz. Vroom," *Jahrbuch der Preussischen Kunstsammlungen,*
1928, pp. 102 ff.
W. Stechow, *op. cit.*
C. van Hasselt, *op. cit.,* p. 174.

This is the same river Spaarne and the same Haarlem with its "Groote Kerk" which Visscher recorded (plate 79). If Visscher had seen Vroom's drawing, he would have wondered why so little of the city itself was shown, and that little set behind a curtain of poplars. Vroom was one of the first to introduce woods into the Dutch scene. His forest landscapes inspired Jacob van Ruisdael, also a Haarlemer. Later, Vroom in turn may have learned from the younger master; but "in contrast to Ruisdael, the main impression remains one of serenity rather than drama or deep solitude" (Stechow, p. 70).

Jan van Goyen
Leiden 1596–1656 The Hague

83. *Two Views of Elterberg*
c. 1650
Black chalk and gray wash, 98 × 157 mm (3 7/8 × 6 3/16″)
Smith College Museum of Art, Northampton, Mass. Gift of Mr. and Mrs.
David F. Seiferheld, No. 1963:43 TR 1160

BIBL. : C. Dodgson, "A Dutch Sketch-Book of 1650," *Burlington Magazine,* 1918, pp. 234 ff.
H. U. Beck, "Jan van Goyens Handzeichnungen als Vorzeichnungen," *Oud Holland,* 1957,
pp. 241 ff.

The contrast to the preceding drawings is striking. Here are the saturated atmosphere, the pervasive animation which fill Van Goyen's country. He leads to the second period of Dutch landscape.

The tiny sheet is from a dismembered sketchbook of nearly three hundred pages. Van Goyen carried such books on his travels, which occasionally took him some distance away from home. The hilly region around Arnhem, at the broad Lower Rhine, attracted him in particular. Elterberg is located between Emmerich and Arnhem.

The books contain sketches of open country, villages, houses, ships, and sometimes groups of peasants. But he seldom used them in his finished works; they rather served as a vocabulary and a reminder. The pages are without the clouds and birds, the bustling activities which fill the paintings as well as those drawings which he made for sale. Yet also such unpretentious notes, done in front of the motifs, carry us right into the life of land and people, and let us join the artist in his wanderings.

The suggestion of a continuous progression is particularly strong in this sheet which shows the same locality twice, from different vantage points. See also Introduction, p. 21.

Jan van Goyen

84. *The River De Vliet, with the House "Hofwijk," near The Hague*
Signed "VG 1653"
Black chalk and gray wash, 181 × 287 mm (7 1/8 × 11 5/16")
Museum Boymans-van Beuningen, Rotterdam, No. H. 101

BIBL. : Exhibition Catalogue, *Dutch Drawings, Masterpieces of Five Centuries,* Washington, D.C.,
1958/59, No. 51.

Larger and more elaborate than the preceding sheet, this drawing was intended for sale. The locality is real: the manor house in the back is Hofwijk, the countryseat of Constantijn Huyghens, statesman, poet, and patron of the arts.* The place as such, however, means little here; the impression of reality stems entirely from an intrinsic liveliness, which carries everything along, nature and man alike.

Jan van Goyen "represents the purest phase of Dutch landscape" (Max J. Friedländer). He was a pupil of Esaias van de Velde (plate 78). It is gratifying to follow his development from his teacher's linear and terse style to the rich and fluid orchestration of such a mature work as this.

See also Introduction, p. 21.

* Built 1639/40. The house still exists. I am indebted for this information to Miss H. A. J. Hos, Rijksbureau voor Kunsthistorische Documentatie, The Hague.

Pieter Jansz. Saenredam
Assendelft 1597–1665 Haarlem

85. *View of Assendelft*
Signed "den 15 Augustij 1633 van mijn Pieter Saenredam tot Assendelft,
   naer 'tleven geteeckent"
Pen and watercolor, 230×385 mm (9 1/16×15 1/4")
Kupferstichkabinett, Staatliche Museen, West Berlin, No. 5704

BIBL. : Exhibition Catalogue, *Pieter Jansz. Saenredam,* Utrecht, 1961, No. 16.

I include a work by Saenredam with some hesitation. He was not a landscapist, but a painter of architecture: mostly interiors of churches which he depicted with a meticulous accuracy and with a surprising perceptiveness for medieval styles.

The purpose of this drawing certainly was to present the Church of Saint Odulphus. Yet, each work of art reveals the peculiar mind of its epoch. And Saenredam would not be of the seventeenth century if he did not relate more than the bare facts of topography. The dreamy village under the summer sky—the only live creature seems to be the stork on the gable—has the homogeneous ambience which fills the landscapes of Jan van Goyen. Saenredam's art differs in his personal blend of observant detachment and intensity.

To our knowledge, the drawing was not used for a painting. In 1813, the church of Assendelft was struck by lightning and burned down.

Assendelft.

Den 15. augusti 1633.
van mij pieter Sar.... ...
tot Assendelft, naer 't leben geteekent.

Aert van der Neer
Amsterdam 1603–1677 Amsterdam

86. *A Fishing Village, at Night*
Signed "AVDN"
Brush in bister, heightened in white, 214×385 mm (8 3/8 × 15 1/8")
Collection F. Lugt, Institut Néerlandais, Paris, No. J. 1770

BIBL. : W. Stechow, *op. cit.*
C. van Hasselt, *op. cit.,* No. 109.

Aert van der Neer's favorite subjects were scenes of winter and of moonlight. About six hundred paintings are listed by Hofstede de Groot, but the copious production seems to have met with little response for the artist lived in poverty. His drawings are rare; their technique and layout are as elaborate as those of paintings.

Stechow, in characterizing the master's style and development, makes the provocative suggestion that the moonlit landscapes were inspired by Rubens. If so, they are translated into a language that is thoroughly Dutch. The moist uniform atmosphere, the silent hour of the night have taken over here; *they* carry the suspense—if "suspense" it can be called.

Simon de Vlieger
Rotterdam 1600/5–1653 Weesp

87. *A Sailboat on the Shore*
Black chalk and gray wash, 160 × 287 mm (6 5/16 × 11 1/4")
Collection F. Lugt, Institut Néerlandais, Paris, No. J. 4489

BIBL. : K. G. Boon and L. C. J. Frerichs, Exhibition Catalogue, *Dessins Hollandais du Siècle d'Or,*
Brussels, 1961, No. 45.
W. Stechow, *op. cit.*

Simon de Vlieger specialized in marines, but he also painted and drew landscape, genre, portraits, and animals.

The seascape speaks for itself. The way in which the beached vessel and the sailors are set against the low horizon, and the way a huge space is suggested with few means, display an ingenuity that is exceptional even for this versatile master.

The drawing seems to date from the 1630s, when De Vlieger painted beach scenes where the sky fills most of the picture.

Rembrandt Harmensz. van Rijn
Leiden 1606–1669 Amsterdam

88. *A Village Before a Thunderstorm*
c. 1635/36
Pen, washes in bister and Chinese ink, 182 × 245 mm (7 1/8 × 9 5/8″)
Albertina, Vienna, No. 8880

BIBL. : O. Benesch, *The Drawings of Rembrandt,* London, 1954–57, No. 800.

Rembrandt's art extends over many fields: portraits, sacred and secular history, mythology, genre, animals, still life, and landscape. Of these subjects, two occupied him at all times: Biblical stories, for they were constantly in his mind; and portraiture, which was his bread and butter. Much can be learned about Rembrandt's train of thought from his taking up or abandoning certain subjects.

Landscape is a case in point. His first landscape, a painting, dates from 1636—ten years after he began his career as an artist. From then on, he occasionally sketched farmhouses and trees, but only in the 1640s did nature become a regular pursuit, and mainly in etching and drawing.

This sheet is an early example. It looks strange amongst its Dutch contemporaries. Rembrandt seems to impose here the dramatic suspense of his religious events upon another field which was new to him. Attention is focused on the cottages, glaringly lighted before the coming storm; one scarcely notices the women in the corner and the swallow on the roof.

See also Introduction, p. 21.

Rembrandt

89. *The Bend in the Amstel River*
c. 1650/51
Reed pen and washes in bister and India ink, some heightening in white,
  136×250 mm (5 5/16×9 13/16″)
Collection Duke of Devonshire, Chatsworth, No. 1021 (Reproduced by
  permission of the Trustees of the Chatsworth Settlement)

BIBL.: F. Lugt, *Mit Rembrandt in Amsterdam,* Berlin, 1920, p. 112.
  O. Benesch, *op. cit.,* No. 1265.

As our selection is limited, it concentrates on the years around 1650 when Rembrandt was most absorbed by nature. The majority of landscape drawings date from that time. During the 1640s, his approach changed; the gradual stages can be followed in the etchings. *The Three Trees* (1643), confronting an approaching shower, still has the tension of the *Cottages,* but *Six's Bridge* (1645) looks calmly around over the flat country.

In this drawing, five years later, everything is fused into a comprehensive whole, an indivisible unity has been achieved. But not a unity of monotonous sameness. The way in which the water adjoins the land, how the sunlight lies upon the ground, or how the riders move away—this is both concordant and diverse, tranquil as well as momentous. One senses that the landscape conveys a message, and one wishes to understand Rembrandt's arcane language more clearly.

The house, visible behind the trees, is the manor of Kostverloren, a landmark near Amsterdam often depicted by the artist.

See also Introduction, p. 21.

Rembrandt

90. *The Nieuwe Meer(?), with a Sailing Boat*
c. 1649/50
Pen and brush in bister, 88 × 181 mm (3 7/16 × 7 1/4")
Collection Duke of Devonshire, Chatsworth, No. 1034 (Reproduced by
   permission of the Trustees of the Chatsworth Settlement)

BIBL. : F. Lugt, *op. cit.*, p. 155.
   O. Benesch, *op. cit.*, No. 847.

No other master makes landscape conform so thoroughly to our own being. We are "in" this country; it seems to have the same rhythm as our soul, and we feel its quiet life as if it were our own. Rembrandt also appeals to our acoustic sense. We believe we hear the water lapping at the shore, the breeze moving over the rushes and, above all, we listen to the silence which reigns in the wide land.

Lugt tentatively identified the site as the Nieuwe Meer, which was an inland body of water near Amsterdam. The slack sail and stay indicate that there is only a slight wind.

See also Introduction, p. 22.

Rembrandt

91. *A Farmhouse Amidst Trees, on the Bank of a Canal*
c. 1651/52
Pen and brush in Chinese ink, 156×233 mm (6 1/8×9 1/8″)
British Museum, London, No. 1895.0.15.1259

BIBL. : O. Benesch, *op. cit.,* No. 1244.

Because Rembrandt's insight progresses constantly and his art changes from year to year, the student never lacks internal evidence for dating his works. But a thorough knowledge of the *oeuvre* and a keen eye are required to arrive at reliable conclusions; even the best experts are sometimes mistaken. I believe that the *Nieuwe Meer* antedates the *Bend in the Amstel,* but do not feel competent to say so with certainty. I am fairly convinced, however, that this drawing is a few years later than both. The mirror-like surface of the water, the sunlight on foliage and ground, betoken a greater luminosity; the complex of houses and trees has a clarity and distinction that were at the master's disposal only after 1650.

See also Introduction, p. 22.

Rembrandt

92. *View of the Amstel; Amsterdam in the Distance*
c. 1653/54
Reed pen in bister, some white gouache, 146×273 mm (5 3/4×10 3/4″)
Kupferstichkabinett, Staatliche Museen, West Berlin, No. 5212

BIBL. : Benesch, *op. cit.*, No. 1352.

The space is indivisible as in the preceding drawings, but the decided verticals, the solemn mood, point toward the mid-fifties. Rembrandt then moved to new and commanding expressions, such as the painting of *Aristotle* (1653) or the etchings of the young Christ (1654). The youth in front, set off against the water and the vast sky (how suggestive can emptiness be!), has a roughhewn look. Significantly, a reed pen is used, in broad and angular strokes.

In those years, landscape became rarer; it no longer seemed adequate for what Rembrandt had to say. Toward 1660, it disappeared entirely from his work.

Rembrandt

93. *A Huntsman Resting in Mountainous Country*
c. 1649/50
Pen in bister, 205 × 198 mm (8 1/16 × 7 3/4")
Present whereabouts unknown

BIBL. : O. Benesch, *op. cit.,* No. 637.

From his youth, Rembrandt was familiar with Italianate landscape through his teacher Lastman, from works of Elsheimer and others, as well as from Venetian prints and drawings. He owned and reworked a drawing by Domenico Campagnola (Benesch, No. 1369). In many of his Biblical stories, southern-style landscapes provide the oriental or ancient background. A number of paintings display mountains and precipices of classical tradition, and fantastic buildings. In etchings or drawings of landscape, however, the country is Holland. Rembrandt kept the two genres apart. Only from 1650 on, there appears in some etchings a high mountain or a huge tower which cannot have sprung from Dutch soil.

Although this sheet is not "pure" landscape, it is reproduced to show how nature and living creatures are attuned to each other. The mountain stands unconcerned yet protective over the resting group; conversely the hunter and hounds impart to the landscape a spirit of adventure and of untraveled expanses.

The huntsman may be the Biblical Nimrod. Rembrandt had a particular fondness for wayfarers in foreign lands: the Archangel Gabriel with the young Tobit, the lean and wiry Mercury, the "Polish Rider."
See also Introduction, p. 23.

Jan Lievens
Leiden 1607–1674 Amsterdam

94. *The Interior of a Forest, with a Lake and Deer*
Reed pen, 223 × 369 mm (8 3/4 × 14 9/16″)
Kunstmuseum, Düsseldorf, No. FP 5086

BIBL. : I. Budde, *Beschreibender Katalog der Handzeichnungen in der Staatlichen Kunstakademie Düsseldorf,* Düsseldorf, 1930, No. 898.
E. Schaar, Exhibition Catalogue, *Meisterzeichnungen der Sammlung Lambert·Krahe,* Kunstmuseum, Düsseldorf, 1969/70, No. 155.

The young Lievens perhaps met Anthony van Dyck in London—if it is true that he was appointed to the court of Charles I—but he certainly saw Van Dyck's work in Antwerp, where he lived from 1635 to 1643. He returned to Holland in 1644.

Van Dyck's style left its mark upon Lievens. It shows in the dignified attitudes of the sitters in his portraits and, I think, also in his landscape drawings. The handwriting of this sheet stems from Van Dyck (plate 74), though it is more angular and coarse.

For a change, one enjoys being in a place with a narrower range of vision, and one is content to stay within the forest. The landscapes of Lievens do not lead the eyes, nor the imagination, very far. These woods cannot elicit thoughts on the age and transience of things, as Ruisdael's do. Still, the beech trees, in their stance and spread, have a noble presence.

Lievens frequently used the reed pen, which produces broader effects than the quill, the customary pen of his time. Rembrandt, too, often drew with the reed, or combined reed and quill. In their youth, the artists were friends, both being pupils of Pieter Lastman. Perhaps their use of the same technique is more than coincidental.

Philips Koninck
Amsterdam 1619–1688 Amsterdam

95. *A Plain with Hills and Woods*
Pen in brown and gray bister, some graphite, 174×324 mm
(6 13/16 × 12 3/4")
Museum Boymans-van Beuningen, Rotterdam, No. 4

BIBL. : H. Gerson, *Philips Koninck,* Berlin, 1936.
         W. Stechow, *op. cit.*

Panoramic views over the Dutch plain began with Goltzius, found their greatest expression through Hercules Seghers, and came to maturity with Philips Koninck and Jacob van Ruisdael.

Koninck here shows the river country near Arnhem. From a slight elevation, he looks over the land which spreads in successive layers of depth to the broad horizon. Jan van Goyen often pictured the same region. Koninck does without the sundry activities which enliven the landscapes of the older artist. His country is empty, uniform, and very quiet; the day goes by like a wide and even stream, in a grandly monotonous flow.

Koninck was a follower of Rembrandt, and indebted to the greater master's example of the 1640s. Conversely, works like this drawing, done about 1650, may have influenced Rembrandt—for instance in the etching *The Goldweigher's Field* (Bartsch, 234; 1651).

Some of Koninck's drawings are washed in different colors—paintings in miniature.

Aelbert Cuyp
Dordrecht 1620–1691 Dordrecht

96. *River Landscape*
Black chalk, gray and black wash, 185 × 308 mm (7 3/4 × 12 1/8″)
Kupferstichkabinett, Staatliche Museen, West Berlin, No. 2373

Cuyp was a prominent and versatile landscapist; in a museum, his paintings catch the eye because of the warmth and clarity of their colors. Like Koninck, he belongs to the generation active after mid-century, when Dutch art had attained a high degree of expertness. This can be seen in the cunning layout of the page, in the precision and delicacy of the aerial perspective; but it is also felt in the general air of distinction and fulfillment. The manner in which vessels and figures interrelate, the way the boats cut into the water which stretches across the full width of the page, bespeak a rare skill.

Cuyp liked to apply to his drawings yellow or greenish-yellow washes which carried some of the color of his painting into paper. Although he never went to Italy and his subjects are domestic, he instills land and life with the genial atmosphere which we find in southern landscape. Often, the setting sun illuminates the country with a golden light. People and animals seem to be caught up in contentment. Not without reason, his works were cherished by the English collectors whose taste had been trained by *Seicento* art.

Lambert Doomer
Amsterdam 1624–1700 Alkmaar

97. *A Courtyard at Ehrenbreitstein, near the Rhine*
Inscribed on the back "De Suerbron toe Kobelens" (the mineral well at
   Koblenz)
Pen, brown and gray washes, 232 × 361 mm (9 1/8 × 14 3/16")
Pierpont Morgan Library, New York City, No. I 220A

BIBL. : C. Hofstede de Groot and W. Spiess, "Die Rheinlandschaften von Lambert Doomer,"
   Wallraf-Richartz Jahrbuch, 1926/27, pp. 183 ff.
   H. Dattenberg, "Zur Datierungsfrage von Lambert Doomers Deutscher Reise," *Oud
   Holland*, 1934, pp. 150 ff.

Paintings of Doomer are rare. He is better known through his drawings, mainly those done in France and Italy (1645), and in Germany and Switzerland (some time between 1654 and 1658). They record notable sites and buildings, and also casual scenes, workers in a farmyard, or a passenger boat on the Rhine. Conveniently, they are often inscribed with the name of the locality. Some drawings exist in a second, more elaborate version, probably done later at home. Of our example, such an "édition de luxe" is in Rotterdam (reproduced in Hofstede de Groot and Spiess, p. 189); there the donkey is placed in the center, the dog pushed to the right; a man sits in the corner and drinks from a bottle.

Doomer was a pupil of Rembrandt, and learned from him to shade drawings with deep, transparent washes. But his attitude is altogether different: he is the observant and thoughtful traveler, with an interest in geography, architecture, and local customs. The vineyards, the evening sun on the old fortress, the women at the well—all the many things tell of an untroubled world, and this only shortly after the Thirty Years' War. The mineral spring still exists.

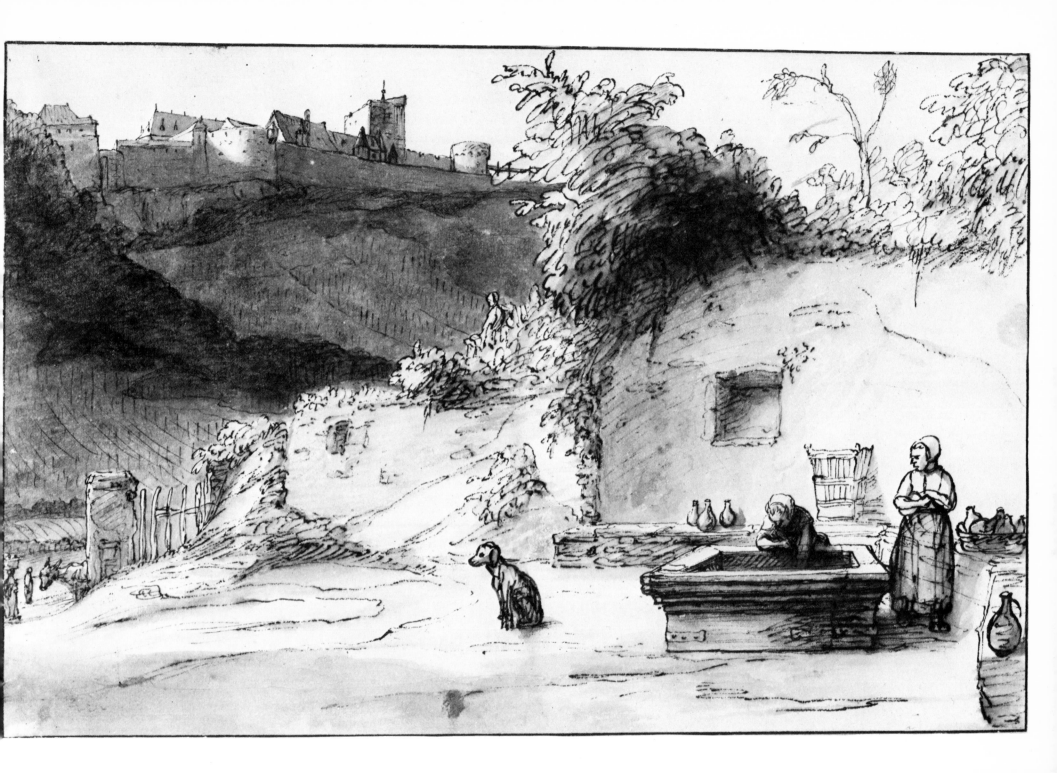

Adam Pynacker
Pijnacker near Delft 1622–1673 Amsterdam

98. *A Bridge in the Countryside near Rome*
Pen, gray wash, heightened in white, 244×368 mm (9 9/16×14 1/2″)
Kupferstichkabinett, Staatliche Museen, West Berlin, No. 3926

BIBL. : Exhibition Catalogue, *Nederlandse 17e Eeuwse Italianiserende Landschapschilders,* Utrecht,
1965, pp. 184 ff.
W. Stechow, *op. cit.*
C. van Hasselt, *op. cit.,* No. 149.

Italianate Dutch landscape has been upgraded by art historians during the last ten years. Will the reevaluation hold good, or is it a passing fashion? Subject matter *per se* has no merit; what is done with it counts; and, in my opinion, none of those Rome-travelers was an eminent master. Berchem and Both, the foremost of them, carry less weight than Cuyp, who never left Holland but who could evoke southern light and a bucolic ambience with more persuasiveness.

In the early decades of the century, Dutch artists helped to create landscape in Italy (e.g., Breenbergh, plate 57). Later, they were rather on the receiving end. This drawing, probably of the 1650s, is indebted to what had been achieved before.

Pynacker, a pupil of Jan Both, lived in Rome from about 1645 to 1648, and, back home again, kept to the Italianizing genre, which was then in demand. He excels in those very features which southern art neglects. His tree trunks, in strong raking light, his surfaces of walls have the detachment of a still life; the later paintings "sometimes exhibit a startlingly near-surrealistic quality" (Stechow, p. 157). This sheet is gratifying by its sober sense, its attention to light-dappled things. That the view is limited to the bridge enhances its charm.

The motif, Ponte di Molo, below Tivoli, may have been drawn from nature, but not necessarily so. It was a well-known site, and appears in drawings by Asselyn, Both, Swanevelt, and also by Claude Lorrain (M. Roethlisberger, *op. cit.,* No. 531).

Jacob van Ruisdael
Haarlem 1628/29–1682 Amsterdam

99. *Mountainous Landscape, with a Brook and a Large Oak*
Inscribed "Ruisdael" by a later hand
Black chalk and gray wash, some heightening in white, 155 × 235 mm
  (6 1/8 × 9 1/4″)
Museum Boymans-van Beuningen, Rotterdam, No. 7

BIBL. : J. Rosenberg, *Jacob van Ruisdael,* Berlin, 1928, No. 68.

Ruisdael's drawings are not numerous. Rosenberg lists about seventy. Most are done in black chalk and gray washes, with dots and short strokes which produce an irregular, bristly texture. The early landscapes are related to those of his uncle Salomon van Ruysdael, and of C. H. Vroom (plate 82). Soon, the younger artist set his own course.

That Jacob van Ruisdael is one of the very great in landscape perhaps sounds overstated. The modern beholder sometimes may feel uneasy in front of the wild scenery, the lonely woods under a dark sky; probably because such motifs were endlessly imitated in later times, and our understanding of Ruisdael is tainted by these derivative repetitions.

If we read him in his own language, a specific and imposing aspect of nature and man-made things comes to light: their growth, their achievement, and also their decline. The tree has reached its height, has spread its roots and branches, the brook has dug its bed. Conversely, a branch has died, the trunk has fallen and decays. Every thing has its history and expresses time's doing and undoing. Hence the tone of awe and resignation in Ruisdael's landscapes. They are not "huge cloudy symbols of a high romance" (Keats), but tell a substantial story.

Jacob van Ruisdael

100. *The Dunes with Egmond-on-the-Sea*
Inscribed "Jb. Ruisdael" by a later hand
Black chalk and gray wash, 202 × 316 mm (7 15/16 × 12 7/16")
Kunsthalle, Hamburg, No. 1917/106

BIBL. : J. Rosenberg, *op. cit.,* No. 31.
W. Stechow, *op. cit.*

In Ruisdael's early work, flat landscapes are rare; he preferred mountainous sites. He borrowed Scandinavian rocks and waterfalls from Everdingen's paintings; he even invented a nonexistent height for the *Castle of Bentheim* (Rosenberg, plates 44 and 46). In his later years, he decided that the horizontal can also be eloquent. His paintings of Haarlem standing within the wide plain have a grandeur which is the more impressive for not being obvious. Egmond, its houses crouching around the Gothic church, had been one of Ruisdael's early subjects. That it is now seen from the distance, very small within the huge space, lends it an enhanced pathos. Unlike Koninck, Ruisdael is mindful of the human condition. He understands the dignity of a city, the isolation of a house, the precarious existence of this town, under the wind that constantly sweeps over the sand and the sparse grass.

The church, already decaying, collapsed in the 1740s (C. van Hasselt, *op. cit.,* No. 5).

Jan de Bisschop
Amsterdam 1628–1671 The Hague

101. *The Village of Scheveningen, from the South*
Pen, brown and blue washes, 165 × 406 mm (6 1/2 × 16″)
British Museum, London, No. 1861.8.10.57

In a more cheerful vein than Ruisdael's dunes, the landscape enchants us by its delicacy and brilliance. The reproduction attempts to render the warm reddish-brown ink, applied in varying shades. It was the artist's own mixture—"Bisschops Inkt," made perhaps with an addition of rust or ground-up red chalk—which gives to his drawings their particular luster.

Bisschop was not a professional artist but a learned amateur. After taking a degree in law, he traveled in Italy, and later became an attorney at The Hague. His artistic interests were manifold: he copied Roman antiquities and the works of the old masters, he drew fantastic allegories, portraits, and landscapes.

Scheveningen and its dunes are a few miles distant from The Hague.

Antoine Watteau
Valenciennes 1684–1721 Paris

102. *A Valley with Houses, Behind Trees*
Red chalk, 160 × 280 mm (6 5/16 × 11″)
Musée Fabre, Montpellier, No. 870–1–80

BIBL. : K. T. Parker and J. Mathey, *Antoine Watteau, Catalogue complet de son oeuvre dessiné,* Paris, 1957, No. 477.
J. Mathey, *Antoine Watteau, Peintures réapparues; . . . ,* Paris, 1959.
M. P. Eidelberg, "Watteau's Use of Landscape Drawings," *Master Drawings,* V, 1967, pp. 173 ff.

The findings of Mathey (1959) and others have shed new light on Watteau's beginnings. In groping for his way, he studied and imitated Titian, Veronese, Rubens, Teniers, Le Nain, even Rembrandt—widely different masters, and all of bygone times. No link exists to the court painting of his time, only to the minor genre of the theater and of decoration which he raised to greatness.

His drawings of landscape fall into two groups. The majority are copies after the old masters, mainly Venetian; the others—about three dozen by present count—are records from nature. Probably all were done for potential paintings, although Watteau seldom used drawings of landscape literally in finished works as he did with studies of human figures.

This sheet may represent the valley of the Bièvre, south of Paris, but it was hardly meant as a topographical account. It rather conveys the imaginary ambience of the parks which surround his fêtes galantes.

Watteau was a native of Valenciennes, thus of a province bordering the Netherlands. The tradition of Rubens is still alive in these rolling hills, curving trees, and the soft foliage.

Antoine Watteau

103. *Houses and Trees on a Road*
Red chalk, 145 × 207 mm (5 11/16 × 8 1/8″)
Musée Bonnat, Bayonne, No. 1719

BIBL. : Parker and Mathey, *op. cit.,* No. 475.

Watteau's mature work gives no hint of his early eclecticism. It expresses fully the concept of French eighteenth-century art; Watteau was its first and most endearing master. As the Goncourts said, he and Fragonard are the true and only poets of all the *dixhuitième*.

It would require an ample choice of drawings, including figures and heads, to show the spectrum of Watteau's art, its exquisite nuances and its perfection. Yet even in this one landscape one feels an almost magic immediacy. The hamlet stands there, fleeting and durable, as if evoked out of nowhere. The drawing speaks in such a clear voice that one is hardly aware of the sublimation which has been achieved.

The sheet may be from the same time as the preceding one, about 1715.

Hubert Robert
Paris 1733–1808 Paris

108. *Temple of Jupiter Serapis in Pozzuoli near Naples*
1759
Red chalk, 329×460 mm (12 15/16×18 1/8″)
Albertina, Vienna, No. 12738

BIBL. : O. Benesch, *Meisterzeichnungen der Albertina,* Salzburg, 1964, No. 221.

To discern the hands of Fragonard and Robert from the years of their companionship is an entertaining and sometimes puzzling business. In most cases, there can be little doubt which of the two is the author. Robert's wrist seems to have moved more abruptly, his strokes are less flexible than Fragonard's, and the pages have a coarser appearance.

Robert's personages are pointedly "people," of specific stations, occupations, and manners. He has a preference for simple folk, and likes to contrast them to the ancient monuments amongst which they move and live. The young women denote the lively and humble present, unconcerned with the dead and august past.

The drawing was made for the Abbé de Saint-Non, who published his etching after it in the *Voyage Pittoresque dans les Royaumes de Naples et des Deux Siciles.*

Robert himself is aware of historical greatness, and the surname "Robert des Ruines" fits his art well. He returned to Paris in 1765, much later than his friend Fragonard. In 1770, he was appointed designer of the king's gardens, a position which ideally suited his experience.

Jean-Jacques de Boissieu
Lyon 1736–1810 Lyon

109. *A Village with a Gothic Church in the Mountains*
Signed "JB" and dated 1782
Brush in black and gray, 164×232 mm (6 7/16×9 1/8")
British Museum, London, No. 1910-2-12-85

BIBL. : Exhibition Catalogue, *Jean-Jacques de Boissieu,* Musée de l'Ain, Bourg-en-Bresse, 1967.

Boissieu lived and worked outside the mainstream. With the exception of a few years in Paris and a journey to Italy, he remained in Lyon, where he became *Conseiller du Roi* and one of the founders of the local Salon.

His main field was etching, in a clever adaptation of the technique of the Dutch. He made prints after the paintings of Ruisdael, Claude Lorrain, and others. His own landscapes combine both southern and northern types.

He is an eclectic artist, to be sure, yet one ought not to underrate him, nor the high level of skill and taste in the remarkable age that gave distinction to its *petits maîtres,* too. A drawing like this one enchánts us in its accomplished layout and cunning use of washes, which catch the most delicate nuances of surface and shading. The serene temper brings to mind Italianate landscapes of the preceding century, but there is an acuity and immediacy in the play of light that belong only to the *dixhuitième*.

The village is probably located in the Alpine region near Lyon. If the church still stands, the place could surely be identified.

Giovanni Battista Tiepolo
Venice 1696–1770 Madrid

110. *A Stone Gate and Farm Buildings*
1755/60
Pen and brush, 142 × 252 mm (5 9/16 × 9 15/16″)
Fitzwilliam Museum, Cambridge, England, No. PD 30 1959 (Reproduced
   by permission of the Syndics of the Fitzwilliam Museum)

BIBL. : A. Rizzi, Exhibition Catalogue, *Disegni del Tiepolo,* Udine, 1965, Nos. 102–7.

Turning from France to Italy again, to the new flowering of Venetian art, one is struck by the deep-rooted differences that exist among the European nations. Tiepolo does not share the attitude of the French, which, broadly speaking, is rational and often critical. He affirms the world unstintingly and brings forth its generous beauty.

Within this eminent artist's far-flung activities, landscape takes a very small place: a few drawings, which are not more than vignettes of thought and observation. Still, such abbreviated notations tell a great deal. In the rusticated stones, a grand realm of architecture lights up, the walls and roofs bespeak the rural outdoors, and the whole evokes a wide and brilliant land under an equally brilliant blue sky. The beholder takes his stand in the middle, his imagination ranges upward and all around. May we say that the stone balls are almost symbolic of the spherical space-concept of the master?

Rizzi places the drawing in the time when Tiepolo worked in Udine, that is, in 1759.

Antonio Canaletto
Venice 1697–1768 Venice

III. *Panorama of a Village*
Signed on the back "Ant. Canal FECIT" and dated 1742
Pen over red crayon, 143 × 394 mm (5 5/8 × 15 1/2")
Fogg Art Museum, Harvard University, Cambridge, Mass. Bequest of
Charles Alexander Loeser Esq., No. 1932.330

BIBL. : A. Mongan and P. J. Sachs, *Drawings in the Fogg Museum of Art,* Cambridge, Mass., 1946, No. 307.
T. Pignatti, *Il Quaderno di Disegni del Canaletto alle Gallerie di Venezia,* Milan, 1958.
T. Pignatti, "Canaletto and Guardi at the Cini Foundation," *Master Drawings,* I, No. 1, 1963, pp. 49 ff.

As this book tries to prove, the story of view-painting cannot be separated from that of landscape in general. It would be idle to determine where recording of facts ends and where fantasy begins.

Canaletto, the foremost of the *vedutisti,* gave to his genre a rank it did not have before. His paintings and finished drawings catered to the demand of the wealthy foreigners, especially the British, who wanted to bring home souvenirs of their Grand Tour.

The drawing represents Padua. It is the right half of a panorama, the left part of which is in the Morgan Library. From this preliminary outline, Canaletto elaborated sections in drawing (Windsor), etching, and painting. He transformed the place considerably; he made the houses higher and ranged them more closely, he added a large foreground which he enlivened with trees and figures (one painting reproduced in Mongan-Sachs, Vol. I, p. 155).

There has been much discussion concerning Canaletto's employment of the *camera obscura* (Pignatti, 1963, p. 52, n. 2). As Pignatti has demonstrated, its use was limited; and it is rather irrelevant for the significance of Canaletto's art, as will be seen from the following note.

Antonio Canaletto

112. *Venice, the Western End of the Canal Grande (Santa Chiara District)*

c. 1729
Pen in black and brown over pencil; pricked, 199×271 mm
(7 13/16×10 5/8″)
Royal Library, Windsor Castle, No. 7476 (Reproduced by gracious permission of Her Majesty the Queen)

BIBL.: K. T. Parker, *The Drawings of Canaletto . . . at Windsor Castle,* London, 1948, No. 13.
T. Pignatti, *op. cit.,* 1958.
W. G. Constable, *Canaletto,* Oxford, 1962.

Prior to making this drawing, Canaletto recorded the row of houses on eight pages of a sketchbook, where he put down all the details of windows, balconies, and chimneys (Museum Correr, Venice; Pignatti, plates 29v to 33r). One would expect such first diagrams to have a stronger immediacy than the finished product done in the shop. Just the contrary is true: only this elaboration, partly drawn with the ruler and executed in various fine pens, differently sharpened, achieves the close tissue of stone-fronts, water, air, traffic that fully conveys the aim of the artist.

The spectacle appears oddly remote, as if separated from us by an invisible screen. More than a visual impression, it evokes something of the life of the city, an hour from its day. Intentionally a *veduta,* without any of the famous landmarks, has been reproduced here because this inconspicuous section of the Canal may illustrate more convincingly the inimitable ambience in Canaletto's world, its blend of factuality and mirage. We still like to see the Venetian scene through his eyes.

The same view exists in three paintings (Constable, 266–68), all in England. This drawing, no less complete, came into the Royal Collection through the artist's famous patron, the Consul Joseph Smith.

Francesco Guardi
Venice 1712–1793 Venice

113. *View of Valsaguna*
1778
Pen, India ink wash, 306×532 mm (12 1/16×20 15/16″)
Collection J. Byam Shaw, London

BIBL. : J. Byam Shaw, *The Drawings of Francesco Guardi,* London, 1951.
   F. Haskell, "Francesco Guardi as *Vedutista* and Some of His Patrons," *Journal of the Warburg Institute,* 1960, pp. 256 ff.
   K. T. Parker and J. Byam Shaw, Exhibition Catalogue, *Canaletto and Guardi,* Venice, 1962, No. 109.
   D. Mahon, "When did Francesco Guardi Become a *Vedutista?*" *Burlington Magazine,* 1968, pp. 69 ff.

At the age of forty or thereabouts, Guardi turned from religious paintings to *vedute,* in the hope of securing a better income. Probably it was Canaletto, then famous, who schooled him in his new line. Guardi's slant, however, is quite different from his tutor's: he builds higher and steeper, his architectures assume quasi-organic inflections, the water stretches into expressive horizontals. Moreover, Guardi liked to depict unusual contemporary events, and with an emphasis on the momentary that is his unique touch.

This large sheet was done on Guardi's last trip to his family home in the Val di Sole between Bassano and Trento. In the late drawings, "the pen seems to flutter over the paper like a winged insect hardly confined to earth, and produces by its very inconstancy a magical effect of light and air" (Shaw, 1951, p. 36).

Guardi's style is that of the high Rococo, which, paradoxically, was already out of fashion then. His clientele was no longer that of Canaletto, but a relatively small number of connoisseurs, mostly Italians (Haskell).

Alexander Cozens
Russia c. 1717–1786 London

114. *Cloud Formations Above a Hilly Country*
Gray and black washes on thin India paper, 216×317 mm (8 1/2 × 12 1/2″)
Collection Mr. D. L. T. Oppé and Miss Armide Oppé, London

BIBL. : A. P. Oppé, *Alexander and John Robert Cozens,* Cambridge, Mass., 1954.
E. H. Gombrich, *Art and Illusion,* New York, 1960, pp. 183 ff.
H. W. Janson, " The 'Image made by Chance' in Renaissance Theory," in *Essays in Honor of E. Panofsky,* New York, 1961, pp. 264 ff.

Alexander Cozens was the son of a British shipbuilder employed in Russia, had a brief schooling in Rome from Horace Vernet (the French marine painter), and then settled in England in 1746. He made his livelihood as instructor at Eton; he also taught drawing to the young princes and princesses at Windsor Castle.

Cozens is a puzzling outsider. In subject and composition, his landscapes are of the generic classicist type; but he had an uncanny genius in fashioning patterns which produce an odd, almost unreal effect, very appealing to the modern eye. He also had an uncommon curiosity about clouds, whose various shapes he studied and classified. Was there a measure of genuine greatness in Cozens, or the rationalizing bent of the eighteenth century, carried to the point of freakishness?

The artist devised an ingenious system of teaching, based on the making of landscape drawings from inkblots smeared haphazardly upon the paper. By having the pupils work from such chance forms, he hoped to stimulate their imagination and force them to hold to the overall composition instead of getting lost in detail. Many theories have since been built on this method, but is it worthy of being linked to Leonardo da Vinci's remarks on images created by chance?

Thomas Gainsborough
Sudbury 1727–1788 London

115. *Wooded Hills with a Pond, Cattle, and a Huntsman*
Black chalk, stumped in various areas; heightened in white chalk,
213 × 323 mm (8 3/8 × 12 3/4")
British Museum, London, No. 1910–2–12–251

BIBL. : M. Woodall, *Gainsborough's Landscape Drawings,* London, 1939, No. 165.

British painting was relatively uncreative for centuries. When, in the eighteenth, it began to assert itself, it used the language of Continental art. Gainsborough looked back to Van Dyck, Ruisdael, Dughet, and, of more recent times, Watteau. His teacher Gravelot was a Frenchman.

What is Gainsborough's personal contribution? An answer cannot be expected from a single piece. One is first captivated by his resourceful technique, by the delicate surface, its shimmer of light and dark. Then one wonders whether the evenness and harmony are not too perfect. Britishers assure us that such landscapes reflect the local charm of Suffolk country, where the artist was born. Yet the impression persists that his lyricism is unspecific and somewhat contrived, that a generic ideal of arcadian beauty and rural bliss has been illustrated.

A student whose taste has been formed by Continental standards has a handicap in a fair appreciation of English art. It often seems to express notions which originally were literary or philosophical, and were only subsequently transposed into visual form.

William Blake
London 1757–1827 London

116. *Dante and Vergil Ascending the Mountain of Purgatory
(Purgatorio IV)*
Inscribed "P-g-Canto 4"
1824/27
Pen over pencil, brush and watercolor, 520×370 mm (20 1/2 × 14 9/16")
Tate Gallery, London

BIBL. : A. S. Roe, *Blake's Illustrations to the Divine Comedy*, Princeton, 1953, p. 142.

The illustration of the *Divine Comedy* was Blake's last commission. It remained unfinished; only seven of the one hundred and two drawings were engraved.

This sheet represents a beardless Vergil, followed by Dante, ascending the mountain.

> We through the broken rock ascended, close
> Pent on each side, while underneath the ground
> Ask'd help of hands and feet.   (30–32)
> . . . .
> I, wearied, thus began: "Parent beloved!
> Turn and behold how I remain alone,
> If thou stay not."   (42–44)

The lines are quoted from Henry Cary's translation, that which Blake used. In the artist's symbolism, the sun is half covered because only in Paradise is the full disk visible. Vergil climbs with his "right" foot, Dante with his left.

Blake's highly charged artistry is not to everybody's liking. One has to believe in him to be receptive to his deliberate mystification. The access is made easier if one places his art within its historical context. Then, the rock will assume that sweep, the clouds the swelling, the entire drawing the animation typical of the eighteenth century.

John Constable
East Bergholt 1776–1837 London

117. *View of East Bergholt over the Kitchen-Garden of Golding Constable's House*
Inscribed on the back of the mount "From the Garden" over an inscription
  by the artist "The Garden belonging to G. Constable Esq."
1812/16
Pencil, 302 × 449 mm (11 7/8 × 17 11/16")
Victoria and Albert Museum, London, No. 623–1888

BIBL. : G. Reynolds, *Victoria and Albert Museum, Catalogue of the Constable Collection,* London,
  1960, No. 176.
  G. Reynolds, *Constable, The Natural Painter,* London, 1965.

Constable's works often are painted ideas, but he knew how to bring them into genuine visual form, and *his* Suffolk therefore looks authentic.

He never left England and preferred to select his motifs within a few miles of his native Dedham—for a good reason. He wanted to paint what he *knew:* his village and valley, its weather and vegetation, the work on the canal and in the fields. Once we are aware of this store of intimate knowledge, and of the attachment involved, the country becomes meaningful. We see this garden through Constable's experience, and fences and paths, fruit trees and elms, the brick wall, the farmhands and the warm sunshine become familiar and gratifying.

Paintings of the same view exist, but the drawing can be considered a finished work. It dates from the beginning of the master's middle period, his best.

With Constable, English painting enters the nineteenth century, and on a high level. He belongs to the discoverers of a new "reality." Understandably, his landscapes made an impact upon Delacroix and Corot.

Joseph Mallord William Turner
London 1775–1851 Chelsea

118. *Saint Gotthard Pass with the Devil's Bridge*
c. 1815
Pen and brush in sepia, 215 × 254 mm (8 7/16 × 10″)
British Museum, London, CXVIII-S. R.78

BIBL. : A. J. Finberg, *The History of Turner's Liber Studiorum*, London, 1924, No. 78.
A. J. Finberg, *The Life of J. M. W. Turner, R. A.*, Oxford, 1961, pp. 83 ff.

Turner's disposition was the very opposite of Constable's. His was a rambling curiosity, reaching into all directions, and prone to eccentricities. He had a new sense for color and its allusive capacities.

A monochrome drawing is reproduced here; the tone of the original is a warm brown. It was designed for the *Liber Studiorum,* the ambitious project which the young artist started in 1806. The title was adapted from Claude Lorrain's *Liber Veritatis,* but the purpose was different. One hundred mezzotint etchings were to furnish a compendium of landscape in its diverse aspects—domestic and foreign, classical and modern, peaceful and agitated, solitary and populous. The range of his art would be demonstrated, and models for students be set. Turner issued several installments, but abandoned the venture in the 1820s, when his interest turned more and more to problems of color.

This drawing was not reproduced in print. It represents the famous bridge on the road to Saint Gotthard, where Turner had been on his first journey to the Continent, in 1802. The scenery is charged with a stirring, if somewhat declamatory, pathos.

A comparison with Blake is instructive. Turner's mountain, although ten years earlier than that of the older master, has the tangible concreteness of the nineteenth century.

Samuel Palmer
Newington 1805–1881 Red Hill

119. *Valley with a Bright Cloud*
Signed "Samuel Palmer" and dated 1825
Inscribed on the original mount:
"And this our life, exempt from public haunt,
Finds tongues in trees, bookes in the running brookes,
Sermons in stones, and good in everything.
As you like it."
Sepia mixed with gum and varnished, 184×278 mm (7 1/4×10 15/16″)
Ashmolean Museum, Oxford, No. 639

BIBL. : A. H. Palmer, *The Life and Letters of Samuel Palmer*, London, 1892.
G. Grigson, *Samuel Palmer, The Visionary Years*, London, 1947, No. 39.

Shakespeare's lines, which fit almost any landscape, are quoted here with an outright anti-worldly intent.

Palmer, according to his own words, was "saved from the pit of modern art" through his friend Linnell, who introduced him to William Blake in 1824, when he was nineteen. The old sage impressed the beginner deeply.

This is one of several drawings influenced by Blake's woodcuts for Thornton's Vergil; the lines and the surface pattern imitate the texture of prints. Like Blake, Palmer was a "severe outlinist." But here, Blake is transposed into the terms of the new century; the landscape is of a more solid substance and accordingly has a strength appealing even to those who may be reluctant to accept its occultism.

The page, while cunningly laid out, strikes one as curiously imbalanced—as often happens in English art.

Richard Parkes Bonington

Arnold (Nottinghamshire) 1802–1828 London

120. *Two Views of Venice*
Inscribed "S. Marc Venice"
1826
Pencil, 204 × 302 mm (8 1/16 × 11 7/8")
Private collection, England

BIBL. : A. Shirley, *Bonington*, London, 1940, p. 108.

Bonington was in Venice during the early summer of 1826. Very likely, he drew the waterfront from a boat, moving from place to place. The same buildings appear more than once in his continuous panorama.

For a man of only twenty-four, the drawing is impressively skillful and mature. The well-defined distances from viewer to objects, the sober but inquisitive attitude—such qualities must have thrilled the young Corot when he discovered works of Bonington in the window of a dealer in Paris. In fact, Bonington, like Constable, made a strong impression upon the young French artists when his paintings were shown at the Salon of 1824. Had he been accorded a normal life-span, his contribution to British art would have equaled that of Constable and Turner.

Georges Michel
Paris 1763–1843 Paris

121. *A View from Montmartre Toward the North*
Inscribed "Montmartre"
Black chalk, with some watercolor, 180×299 mm (7 1/16×11 3/4")
The Louvre, Paris, No. R. F. 3943 verso

BIBL. : *Inventaire Général des Dessins du Musée du Louvre . . .*, Vol. X, Paris, n. d., No. 9881.
A. Sensier, *Etude sur Georges Michel*, Paris, 1873.
Exhibition Catalogue, *Cent Ans de Paysage Français*, Fontainebleau, 1957.

Georges Michel was a craftsman of landscape. Once we know his manner, we spot his paintings easily. The wide horizons and clouded skies over strongly lighted plains create a dramatic contrast which harks back to Ruisdael.

Born in 1763, Michel straddles the divide between the eighteenth and the nineteenth centuries, and the art historian is uncertain whether this "romanticism" belongs to the old or the new era.

Michel's drawings can be very attractive. Many depict the Parisian *banlieue,* in his time pleasantly rural and vacant. Here, the plain of Saint-Denis is seen from Montmartre, the master's favorite ground. The trees, the winding Seine, the recession into the distance are rendered with a documentary nicety. Still, to my feeling, the page has some of the pliancy of the *dixhuitième,* although it certainly dates from Michel's later years.

Jean-Auguste-Dominique Ingres
Montauban 1780–1867 Paris

122. *The Villa Medici in Rome*
1809/11
Pencil, 183 × 235 mm (7 3/16 × 9 1/4″)
Musée Ingres, Montauban, No. 867.4437

BIBL. : H. Naef, *Rome vue par Ingres,* Lausanne, 1960, No. 25.

It is tempting to compare the *vedute* of Canaletto (plates 111, 112) and Ingres. While a similarity is obvious, they could not be farther apart in spirit. From Ingres' views the animation is gone. The buildings, gardens, and streets are depicted for their identity; one wants to know their names, their location in the topography of Rome.

The young artist drew these souvenirs for himself and a few friends at home. Hence, most of them are still together in the Ingres Museum. The portrait drawings of the same time were mostly done on commission and passed into the hands of the sitters. They are now widely dispersed, and therefore better known. Yet the views of Rome also show the great draftsman breaking away from the *ancien régime*. Without atmosphere, with austere thin lines, they bespeak the new "reality" which Ingres brought about, single-handed and single-minded, in the years of his sojourn in Italy, 1806–24.

When he did this drawing, he was a *pensionnaire* of the French Academy which, since 1803, had been housed at the Villa Medici, on Mount Pincio. The terrace has a superb view of the city. The Villa is seen here from the garden toward the northwest; at the lower left is the Piazza del Popolo.

Caspar David Friedrich
Greifswald 1774–1840 Dresden

123. *The Source of the River Elbe and the Elbgrund*
Dated July 10, 1810
Pencil and watercolor, 250×340 mm (9 13/16×13 3/8″)
Collection Winterstein, Munich

BIBL. : Exhibition Catalogue, *Deutsche Zeichenkunst der Goethezeit*, Graphische Sammlungen, Munich, 1958, No. 41.

The visual art which Germany produced about 1800 cannot measure up to her poetry and philosophy. Yet it was the first time in centuries that painting and drawing found a distinct national voice; the enthusiasm of a renascence is evident in the works of the young generation.

Friedrich was one of its early and foremost members. Born in northern Prussia, a student at the Copenhagen Academy, he became a teacher in Dresden. His landscapes soon attracted attention; Goethe bought some of his drawings. Later, his fame was forgotten and has been revived only in our day.

Friedrich's ideal was twofold: a faithful rendering of nature and, beyond that, an expression of its grandeur and sanctity. This he often tried to achieve by thematic means, bare giant oaks rising toward a huge sky, night wanderers watching the clouds, a lonely figure gazing out to sea. He is at his truest and best when he lets nature speak naturally. In this drawing, the widely stretched slopes have a purity, the small figure at the fountainhead of the Elbe a tone of quietness, which need no "romantic" embellishment.

Ferdinand Olivier
Dessau 1785–1841 Munich

124. *View of the Castle Hohensalzburg and of Salzburg, from the Mönchsberg*
1817/18
Pencil, heightened in white, 262 × 411 mm (10 5/16 × 16 3/16″)
Albertina, Vienna, No. 25354

BIBL.: H. Schwarz, *Salzburg und das Salzkammergut,* 3rd ed., Vienna, 1958, p. 29.

Olivier was born in Dessau, a small town and ducal seat in eastern Germany. First a disciple of Caspar David Friedrich in Dresden, he moved to Vienna in 1811 and thus became the bridge between North German Romanticism and the young "Nazarenes" (Schnorr von Carolsfeld, Overbeck, Pforr, and others). He did not follow this group to Rome, but preferred to stay in Austria.

Just about that time, Salzburg and the Salzkammergut became known to a wider public. Olivier wrote to a friend that the existing "weak topographical prints can give no conception of the greatness and dignity, the grace and variety of these regions, which match even the most beautiful Italian sites." His own drawings do full justice to their beauty; they count among the best landscapes of the time.

The Nazarenes wished to revive the "simple and pious" old German tradition which they sported even in their dress. Indeed, in this drawing, the meticulous technique, the attention to stone and plants, the contrast of foreground and background may recall early German works—although, naturally, it is quite different in concept. One has to look only at the two strollers on the right (Ferdinand's brother with his bride), to realize that their role is not comparable to that of the figures in a sixteenth-century landscape.

Jean-Baptiste-Camille Corot
Paris 1796–1875 Paris

125. *A View of Mount Soracte from Civita Castellana*
Inscribed "Civita Castellana 7bre 1827"
Pen over pencil, 280 × 415 mm (11 × 16 5/16")
Fogg Art Museum, Harvard University, Cambridge, Mass.
Bequest of Meta and Paul J. Sachs, No. 650

BIBL. : A. Mongan and P. J. Sachs, *op. cit.,* Vol. I, p. 348.

In the early nineteenth century, Italy was still the country where the student painter could best learn the norms of his profession. But to a new generation from France and Germany, it was also the land ideally suited for the landscapist, with more distinctive formations and a bluer sky than at home, and where a steadier weather allowed him to put up his easel in *plein-air,* day after day.

Corot came to Rome for the first time in December 1825, and stayed for almost three years. He worked arduously, as the many views of the city and its environs attest. This drawing is one of about two dozen from the region around Civita Castellana. It depicts Mount Soracte, an isolated limestone ridge, on clear days visible from Rome, some forty-five miles away. In front lies the Monastery Sant' Andrea.

The young master's enthusiasm for Italy speaks in the sheet, and no less his keen eye and mind. He noted in his diary "one ought not to leave anything vague" (il ne faut laisser d'indécision en aucune chose).

See also Introduction, p. 27.

civita Castellana 7ber 28 04

Jean-Baptiste-Camille Corot

126. *A Valley near Morestel (Dauphiné)*
Inscribed "Morestel Juillet 1852"
Pencil, 277 × 422 mm (10 7/8 × 16 5/8")
The Louvre, Paris, No. 8868

BIBL. : A. Robaut, *L'Oeuvre de Corot,* Paris, 1905, Vol. I, p. 138; Vol. II, No. 2829.

In the summer of 1852, Corot visited the Dauphiné, in southeastern France, where he met a junior colleague, François Daubigny. The acquaintance was fruitful to both. Corot was already receptive to a broader technique. His landscapes became soft and atmospheric at that time, as comparison with the preceding example shows.

Essentially, Corot always knew his own direction, and he kept aloof from the changing fashions which sprang up during his long life. But it was he who often was asked for advice by younger *confrères,* of such different aspirations as (for instance) Pissarro and Redon.

When we think, in retrospect, of nineteenth-century landscape, Corot's stands out as its most consistent and, perhaps, purest expression. We still like to see the places which he portrayed through his eyes—what greater homage to a landscapist?

See also Introduction, p. 28.

Morestel Sädler 18?

Eugène Delacroix
Charenton-Saint-Maurice (near Paris) 1798–1863 Paris

127. *A Country Road with Trees, in Winter*
c. 1838
Black and white chalk, 263 × 382 mm (10 3/8 × 15 1/16″)
Sterling and Francine Clark Art Institute, Williamstown, Mass., No. 1421

BIBL.ʼ: E. Haverkamp Begemann, S. D. Lawder, and C. W. Talbot, *Drawings from the Clark Art Institute,* New Haven and London, 1964, No. 173.

Uppermost in Delacroix's mind were man and his history. Landscapes are a minor part of his *oeuvre;* he never showed one at the Salon. The remark of his friend Baudelaire may well reflect his own attitude: "I cannot suppress a strong feeling of annoyance when I hear a landscapist . . . talked about with the same emphasis which one would use to praise a universal painter . . ." (*Variétés Critiques*, Paris, 1924, Vol. I, p. 219).

Just the same, the paintings and sketches of nature also reveal the searching and lofty thoughts of the great artist. The bare tortuous shapes of trees, the country lane disappearing behind the slope, the low sky, evoke the sombre mood of a winter day and are as telling as his stories of adventure and tragedy.

Victor Hugo
Besançon 1802–1885 Paris

128. *The "Mouse Tower," near Bingen*
Inscribed "27 7bre 1840. La Tour des Rats. Victor H."
Ink and sepia washes, 280×430 mm (11×16 15/16")
Collection Maison de Victor Hugo, Paris, No. 49

BIBL. : G. Picon, R. Cornaille, and G. Herscher, *Victor Hugo Dessinateur,* Paris, 1963, No. 34.

The Rhine looms large in Victor Hugo's life and work. He visited it repeatedly from 1838 to 1869. In 1842 he published a sequence of letters, *Le Rhin,* in which he wrote: "I love the Rhine of all rivers. It is a noble river, feudal, republican, imperial; worthy to be both French and German" (Letter 14). The "Mäuseturm" was, according to the legend, the last refuge of a cruel bishop who was harassed and finally devoured by mice. Hugo describes how, one evening, he saw the dilapidated tower for the first time: " . . . at my feet, the Rhine, hurrying with a furious murmur, as if running from a misdeed . . . at its right and left, mountains, or rather, obscure masses disappearing in a cloudy sky . . . for horizon, an immense curtain of darkness; in the middle of the stream, upright in the flat waters . . . a big black tower . . . of a horrible shape; its roof emitting some reddish nebulosity . . . no human sound in this solitude, not a single cry of a bird, a glacial and sinister silence, disturbed only by the irritated and monotonous grumble of the Rhine. . . . Before my eyes was the *Mäuseturm*. . . . I had not imagined it so frightening. . . . " (Letter 20). So it goes on for several pages; one can compare the great writer with the bizarre and less voluble draftsman.

Based on a small study done at the spot (Bibliothèque Nationale, Paris, MS, Album 13348, fol. 34), the drawing was probably executed after Hugo returned to Paris.

Moritz von Schwind
Vienna 1804–1871 Munich

129. *A Woman in a Landscape; at the Right,*
the Ruins of a Medieval Castle
Pen and sepia, 233 × 269 mm (9 3/16 × 10 5/8″)
Albertina, Vienna, No. 6527

After the early Nazarenes had had their say, German art became less austere. It settled for the mellower "Biedermeier," of which Schwind is a major spokesman. His art shows the amiable temper of the Austrians; it has great facility and a wide range. He is at his best in illustrations: stories of wayfaring knights, or fairy tales. His forests remain implanted in the German heritage—there is a winsome poetry in the old trees and secret paths, in their real or legendary inhabitants.

The drawing appears demure, but in fact is rather effusive. The artist commits the beholder to the landscape, in the person of the little lady taking her solitary promenade. It is with her pensive mood that he is supposed to contemplate the clouds, the trees, and the ruins.

In comparing Schwind with Hugo, the reader will realize the contrast between the German and the French temperaments.

Adolf Menzel
Breslau 1815–1905 Berlin

130. *A German Village*
Signed "Menzel" and dated 44
Pencil, 211 × 270 mm (8 5/16 × 10 5/8")
Museum of Fine Arts, Budapest, No. 1935–2869

BIBL. : S. Meller, "Handzeichnungen des 19. Jahrhunderts aus der Sammlung Paul von Majovszky," *Die Graphischen Künste,* XLII, Vienna, 1919, p. 46.

As a young man, Menzel had to take over his father's graphic business. His chief commissions during the 1840s were illustrations for books on the history of Frederick the Great. The woodcuts, drawn by the artist himself on the blocks, are technically superb, and show his extraordinary flair for narrative. To make the work historically sound, Menzel documented all available data, down to the buttons on the coats of the Prussian grenadiers. Indeed, "documentation" is a main virtue of Menzel's art. He faithfully records the village, with its timber-frame and plaster houses, the various trees, the old stone bridge, and the weir in the small river. One would like to know the name of the place and the province where it is located. The restrained charm combines well with the graphic perfection of the drawing. The pencil has to give its finest nuances, partly by stumping.

Honoré Daumier
Marseille 1808–1879 Valmondois

131. *A Couple Seated Beneath the Trees*
Signed "H.D."
Pen and brush, 185 × 265 mm (7 1/4 × 10 7/16")
Collection Madame David-Weill, Paris

BIBL. : K. E. Maison, *Honoré Daumier, Catalogue Raisonné of the Paintings, Watercolours and Drawings,* New York, 1968, Vol. II, No. 718 ("En Contemplation").

Daumier was devoted almost exclusively to a single theme: man and the human condition. Is it permitted to class this drawing as a "landscape"? Recalling how others painted a similar subject—Courbet in *Les Demoiselles au Bord de la Seine,* Seurat in *La Grande Jatte*—one may find that nature is of little account to Daumier. Yet it *is* present here, and strongly so; not so much physically as reflected in the bourgeois couple who, for a brief Sunday, have exchanged the streets of Paris for the open country, but still carry the life of the city with them. It is the contrast between the persons and their temporary habitat that makes the comfortable meadow, the coolness of the shade, and the peaceful view relevant.

Théodore Rousseau
Paris 1812–1867 Barbizon

132. *A Group of Oak Trees, with a Farmhouse*
Black chalk, 510 × 650 mm (20 1/16 × 25 9/16")
Collection Dr. Arnold Deuber, Basel

BIBL. : F. Daulte, *Le Dessin Français de David à Courbet,* Lausanne, 1953, No. 44.
R. L. Herbert, Exhibition Catalogue, *Barbizon Revisited,* Boston, 1962.

From mid-century on, we sometimes come across such over-sized sheets as the above, a fact which is not sufficiently explained by the lower price of mass-produced paper, although this counted too. (Michel, as Guardi had done, still saved the wrapping papers of his tobacco for drawing.) Clearly, the giant dimensions of Rousseau's drawing conform to the majesty of his tree. The artist wrote of an encounter with such an oak: "He spread his great arms like an old bard. A branch fell at my feet and nearly killed me; it would have been a beautiful death, in the heart of the forest . . . See all those beautiful trees . . . I made all their portraits" (Herbert, p. 68).

This is nature in a new key, loaded with a primordial, awe-inspiring grandeur. Rousseau explored the forest of Fontainebleau (Barbizon is at its border), the marshes of the Berry, the vast Landes near Bordeaux. He looked not for their local features, but only for nature herself, for her seasons and moods, more often than not a somber mood. Though painted in *plein-air,* his canvases are darkish—"murky," as the critics objected.

The Barbizon masters felt a sacred obligation to be true to nature, even in her physical substance. Millet sometimes mixed sand with his pigments (Herbert, p. 56). The materials of leaves and bark are depicted here with a reverential earnestness.

Jean-Francois Millet
Gruchy (Normandy) 1814–1875 Barbizon

133. *Fields with Peasants Ploughing and Sowing*
Charcoal, 145 × 211 mm (5 11/16 × 8 5/16")
Ashmolean Museum, Oxford

_____

BIBL. : H. L. Herbert, *op. cit.*

Millet, too, is intent upon the concreteness of things: the air is humid, the soil is heavy. To plough means to move clod after clod; the very grains from the sower's hand are counted. Van Gogh, when he copied Millet's painting *The Sower,* noted this well. He also understood the allusion to the parable of the sower in the Gospel.

Unlike Rousseau, Millet gives man a place in nature. His peasants and the earth on which they labor belong to each other. He shows rural life, tells of its drudgery and mute dignity, always with an emphatic fatalism which the beholder of the twentieth century may not care to share. Yet, Millet does not sermonize (as some of the Pre-Raphaelites did); what he believed became a visual image and thus genuine art.

The drawing seems to date from the years about 1855.

Thomas Cole
Bolton-le-Moor (England) 1801–1848 Catskill, New York

134. *Maple, Balsam Fir, Pine, Shaggy Yellow Birch, White Birch*
1828
Pencil, 272 × 368 mm (10 11/16 × 14 1/2″)
The Detroit Institute of Arts, No. 39.196. H, folio 5 B

BIBL. : Exhibition Catalogue, *Thomas Cole, 1801–1848, One Hundred Years Later,* Hartford, Conn. and New York, 1948/49.

A small selection of American drawings is inserted here, at mid-century. If filed chronologically, they would have to be scattered amongst the Europeans. However, the two sides of the Atlantic did not develop at the same pace, and America's contribution will be more telling when considered as a group. Of necessity, American art in the nineteenth century was part of the general Western tradition and was also plagued with the ambition, which had beset European painting since Neo-Classicism, to display exalted events and profound ideas. On the other hand, American art participated eagerly in the discovery of a new reality.

Thomas Cole's suites, *The Course of Empire* (1836), *The Voyage of Life* (1840), are cosmoramas, catering to a popular taste for bombastic and sentimental subjects. His landscape paintings use Italianate devices and motifs which had become clichés long since. One of his pictures is entitled *Salvator Rosa Sketching Banditti*!

But the early drawing reproduced here, not made with an eye to public consumption, shows the artist in a different light. Here is a perceptive grasp of structures, a scrutiny of the different varieties of trees. The detailed inscriptions, for instance, "the lower branches droop more than the upper ones," indicate an almost scientific concern.

The page belongs to a booklet of notes and drawings made on a tour of the White Mountains, October 1828.

39.196.71

John William Casilear
New York 1811–1893 Saratoga

135. *Lake George*
Inscribed "Lake George July 31st '61"
Pencil, 217 × 356 mm (8 9/16 × 14")
Museum of Fine Arts, Boston. M. and M. Karolik Collection, No. 52.1628

BIBL. : *Catalogue M. and M. Karolik Collection of American Water Colors and Drawings,* Boston,
1962, Vol. I, p. 96, No. 115.
S. M. Green, *American Art,* New York, 1966.

Reading the biographies of the "Hudson River School" painters, one has the impression that America gave artists a better break than the European countries did. Landscape paintings were in good demand from cultivated and well-to-do patrons. Moreover, it was easier in the United States to combine an artistic calling with a gainful occupation. Several artists were also graphic craftsmen. Casilear, for example, became so successful as an engraver of bank notes that he could eventually devote himself wholly to painting and drawing.

America offered another opportunity to the landscapist in the immensity and variety of the land and the clarity of the light. Charles Dickens, in his *American Notes* of 1842, remarks of the luminosity that makes objects "bright and twinkling," and recalls an evening when "every sharp outline looked a hundred times sharper than ever" (Green, p. 261).

One will not compare this drawing by a less than prominent artist with a landscape by Corot. Yet, it gives somewhat more than a likeness of Lake George. It conveys its spaciousness and isolation within a vast country, and suggests the limpidity of the water and the quietness of the borders, not yet disturbed by the noise of motors.

Lake George July 31st 61

Thomas Moran
Bolton (England) 1837–1926 Santa Barbara (California)

136. *Grand Canyon, Utah, from Powell's Plateau*
Signed "T. Moran" and dated 1873
Watercolor over pencil, 192×271 mm (7 9/16×10 11/16")
Cooper-Hewitt Museum of Decorative Arts and Design,
   Smithsonian Institute, New York City, No. 1917–17–26

BIBL. : A. Ten Eyck Gardner, "Scientific Sources of the Full-length Landscape; 1850," *Metropolitan Museum of Art Bulletin,* IV, 1945, pp. 59 ff.
   W. Born, *American Landscape Painting,* New Haven, 1948.
   W. H. Gerdts, Exhibition Catalogue, *Thomas Moran,* Riverside, Cal., 1963, No. 9.

The artistic discovery of the West had begun in the 1820s, mainly with a topographical and ethnographical interest. Moran explored the territories systematically and on a large scale. He joined Ferdinand Hayden's expedition to the Yellowstone Valley in 1871 and John Powell's to the Colorado River in 1873. This sheet is a record from the latter. The style has changed since the time of the Hudson River School. It reflects the desire to make "bigger and better" landscapes, and Moran certainly knew how to pull out the stops—he had studied Turner in London. But is it right to call his landscapes "an outright, uninhibited orgy, a pictorial fire music more Wagnerian than Wagner" (Born, p. 109)?

The European dilemma between "romantic" fancy and "realistic" candor seems to be pointless in these mountains. Here, nature *is* fanciful and dramatic, while Turner *makes* it so.

Of course, it is wrong to evaluate landscapes by asking "fact or fantasy?" However, one should not miss the scientific aim of the American landscapists who depicted little-known regions of the new world. Frederick Church, for instance, was stimulated by Alexander Humboldt's *Cosmos.* In his *Heart of the Andes,* he presented in visual terms the South American wilderness which the great scientist had recorded in his book (Gardner). A similar intent must be granted to Moran. His views of the Rocky Mountains form a sort of compendium, and they characterize the landmarks more adequately than photographs can do.

Moran.
1878

Winslow Homer

Boston 1836–1910 Prout's Neck (Maine)

137. *The Pioneer*
Signed "Homer" and dated 1900
Watercolor, 357×533 mm (13 1/2 × 21")
The Metropolitan Museum of Art, New York City. Lazarus Fund,
    No. 10. 228.2

BIBL. : A. Ten Eyck Gardner, *Winslow Homer,* New York, 1961, p. 145.

Homer could have been omitted from this anthology by reasoning that his field was genre not landscape, that his medium was watercolor not drawing. But he must figure here, I think, because his work belongs to the national heritage and ideally represents one current in American art of the past century—optimistic, folksy, somewhat sentimental.

Homer's craftsmanship is remarkable. Although self-taught, he was familiar with Impressionist technique and Japanese patterning, and he bent them to his own needs. One admires the structure of his pages, the virile colors. Yet, to do him justice, one also has to accept his subjects. The storyteller cannot be dissociated from the painter.

Winslow Homer began as an illustrator. Through many years, he supplied the designs for woodcuts in *Harper's Weekly* and other magazines, producing fashionable genre, scenes of farm life (mostly with children), incidents of the Civil War. Later, when he isolated himself in Maine, he turned to weightier themes—the power and weather of the sea, the struggle of man with nature.

To appreciate this view in the Adirondacks, with a lone woodcutter, the reader will recall our remark on Schwind (plate 129). Here, too, nature is seen from man's point of view and in the context of his life. The country, being America, is rough and demanding, with challenges and promises that had vanished long since from the European continent.

In 1900, the date of the watercolor, the pioneering age was already on the way out in the eastern states. To the artist, the scene probably had historical and nostalgic connotations.

Camille Pissarro
St. Thomas Island 1830–1903 Paris

138. *View of La Varenne*
Signed "C. P." and inscribed "La Varenne"
c. 1863
Pen in India ink over pencil, 210 × 362 mm (8 1/4 × 14 1/4")
Private collection

BIBL. : A. Mongan, Exhibition Catalogue, *Drawings from the Collection of Curtis O. Baer,* Cambridge,
Mass., 1958, No. 45.
A. Mongan, Exhibition Catalogue, *French Drawings from American Collections,* Rotterdam,
1958, No. 175.

Concurrent with the fervid art of Barbizon and of Courbet, another cooler trend came forth since the 1850s. It would be a worthwhile task to gather examples of this pre-Impressionist soberness, manifested in early and little known drawings by Boudin, Degas, Jongkind, and others.

Pissarro would figure in that documentation. Born in the West Indies, he came to Paris in 1855, where the diverse and contradictory trends must have been bewildering. Trying to steer his way, the young artist found in Corot an advisor and protector. Indeed, this drawing reflects Corot's early, linear style. Yet with a difference: the suggestion of a specific atmosphere, the overlapping of terrains, the complex shifts of distances aim at a more incidental aspect, and Pissarro seems to have taken a more detached attitude. A new age, with other formulations and connotations, announces itself.

In 1863, Pissarro did several paintings of La Varenne with the river Marne, east of Paris. The notations penciled on this sheet ("gris chaud," "temps chaud—ciel bleu gris chaud," "herbes") indicate that it was sketched for a painting—lost or not carried out.

temps chaud — ciel bleu gris chaud

gris chaud

C.P.

la Varenne

Claude Monet
Paris 1840–1926 Giverny

139. *View of Rouen Across the Seine*
Signed "Claude Monet"
Probably done shortly before 1883
Black crayon on white scratchboard, 327 × 513 mm (12 7/8 × 19 13/16″)
Sterling and Francine Clark Art Institute, Williamstown, Mass., No. 1097

BIBL. : E. Haverkamp Begemann, S. D. Lawder, and C. W. Talbot, *op. cit.,* No. 159.

The large sheet is a copy by Monet after his own painting of 1872. He drew it on scratchboard, a paper with fine grooves, manufactured for reproduction by photogravure. No doubt the artist did the drawing for such a purpose, but no print is known.

This is the only example of Impressionist landscape in our selection. By a skillful gradation in the density and strength of the crayon, Monet achieved a remarkable painterly effect. His comprehension for water and air in all weathers and seasons is apparent also in the black-and-white medium not familiar to him.

It is instructive to compare Monet's Seine with Victor Hugo's Rhine (plate 128), done some forty years earlier.

Claude Monet

Paul Cézanne
Aix-en-Provence 1839–1906 Aix-en-Provence

140. *Landscape near Gardanne*
c. 1885
Pencil and watercolor, 300 × 490 mm (11 13/16 × 19 5/16″)
Collection Mrs. Marianne Feilchenfeldt, Zürich

BIBL. : Exhibition Catalogue, *Paul Cézanne,* Belvedere, Vienna, 1961, No. 55.

In the 1870s, when Cézanne was close to Pissarro, he was already pursuing a kind of clarification different from that of Impressionism. In the early 1880s, he attained his objective.

The distances are gauged here with a marvelous perspicuity. We know the master's working procedure from half-finished landscapes: he painted concurrently in the fore-, middle, and backgrounds, articulating a whole which he had visualized beforehand. The buildings and layers of terrain in this drawing are set into a pre-established space, which comprises the ground and the air. The landscape, while spare, is complete. The beholder's imagination can fill in the variegated country which has not been spelled out.

Gardanne is situated south of Aix. Sir John Evelyn, who traveled through these parts on his Grand Tour, entered in his diary, October 7, 1644: "We had a most delicious journey from Aix to Marseille, through a country sweetly declining to the south and Mediterranean coast, full of vineyards and olive-yards, orange trees, myrtles, pomegranates, and the like plantations, to which belong pleasantly-situated villas . . . in prospect showing as if they were so many heaps of snow dropped out of the clouds among those permanent greens."

See also Introduction, p. 30.

Paul Cézanne

141. *Pistachio Tree at the Château-Noir*
1895–1900
Pencil and watercolor, 535 × 431 mm (21 1/8 × 17")
The Art Institute of Chicago. Ryerson Collection, No. C 12.420

BIBL. : L. Venturi, *Cézanne, son art, son oeuvre,* Paris, 1936, No. 1040.
A. Neumeyer, *Cézanne Drawings,* New York and London, 1958, No. 84.

This watercolor, too, asks to be read three-dimensionally. Each of the four blocks at the bottom lies at a different angle and distance, the trees range in all directions. In the reproduction, the spatial amplitude and clarity do not appear as fully as in the original. The strongest impact stems, of course, from Cézanne's shaping and coordinating the divergent forms. "A precarious balance between wild growth and order is established" (Neumeyer, p. 60).

Venturi's dating, 1895–1900, leaves a rather wide margin, for Cézanne's style changed continuously. Since Venturi's publication, we discern the nuances of the development more sharply; also some dates have been established by external evidence. The scholars who now study the logic of the master's progress anew might some day be able to place a work within a span of about two years.

The Château-Noir is located a few miles east of Aix. It was a new building, in Gothic style. Cézanne had rented a room there for storing canvases and a painting kit.

Paul Cézanne

142. *The Mont Sainte Victoire with the Château-Noir*
Pencil and watercolor, 316 × 487 mm (12 7/16 × 19 3/16″)
Albertina, Vienna, No. 24048

BIBL. : L. Venturi, *op. cit.,* No. 1025.
        Exhibition Catalogue, *Paul Cézanne,* Belvedere, Vienna, 1961, No. 70.

The Mont Sainte Victoire appears in Cézanne's work for the first time about 1867, in the *Railway Cutting* (Munich), where it is not the main feature. Fifteen years later, Cézanne took up the motif again, and from then on it became a constant theme, as the distant and highest point in an extensive country, or the single elevation with a peculiar trapezoidal summit. He painted and drew it from different vantage points, ever trying to bring it to ultimate clarification while knowing that there was no end to that pursuit. In the mid-nineties, Cézanne approached the mountain from nearby, and made it tower with a new eminence. This is the time of our drawing. Here it rises with its cyclopean volume, looming heavily above the lower hills and the building.

But this is not the last version. In Cézanne's latest years, he sets Mont Sainte Victoire in the midst of a horizontal plain, a right-angled triangle whose left shoulder rises in a long straight line, while the right drops abruptly, almost overhanging the plain.

When a visitor drives out from Aix, curious to meet the mountain "in person," he is surprised that it consists of real stone with a varied surface, and is a normal, if signal, part of the country. He realizes that it was the master who gave it its true personality.

See also Introduction, p. 29.

Odilon Redon
Bordeaux 1840–1916 Paris

143. *A Tree in the Clearing of a Forest*
Black chalk and charcoal, 510 × 360 mm (20 1/16 × 14 1/8″)
Rijksmuseum Kröller-Müller, Otterlo, No. 642

BIBL. : R. Bacou, *Odilon Redon,* 2 Vols., Geneva, 1956.
R. Bacou, Exhibition Catalogue, *Odilon Redon,* Orangerie, Paris, 1956/57, No. 9.
J. Rewald, Exhibition Catalogue, *Redon Moreau Bresdin,* New York, 1962.
L. Nochlin, *Impressionism and Post-Impressionism 1874–1904, Sources and Documents,* Englewood Cliffs, N. J., 1966, pp. 191 ff.

During all the nineteenth century, diverging tendencies existed simultaneously. Redon, in age equal to Cézanne, Monet, Renoir, Sisley, took an entirely different course. His "symbolism" has often been misunderstood. A sharp line has to be drawn between his sophisticated ambivalence and a blurred mysticism. Redon's art, like the poetry of his friend Mallarmé, is cerebral. The sarcastic remarks which the artist penciled on the margins of a nebulous eulogy by Emile Bernard (Bacou, Vol. I, 1956, pp. 274 ff.) are amusing, and a chastening lesson to any overeager interpreter.

Redon's landscapes are less fantastic than the heads and monsters to which he owes his fame. Still, this tree looks chimerical; its outlandish charm is the more alluring for remaining unexplained.

The page shows the master's devotion to the "noirs" of the charcoal; black to him was the most essential color, which "derives its exaltation and its life, undeniably, from the profound . . . sources of health. . . . nothing can degrade it . . . black is the medium of the mind. . . . " (Nochlin, pp. 196–97).

Georges Seurat
Paris 1859–1891 Paris

144. *The Island of La Grande Jatte*
1884/85
Conté crayon, 400×602 mm (15 3/4×23 11/16″)
Private collection, New York

BIBL. : D. C. Rich and R. L. Herbert, Exhibition Catalogue, *Seurat,* Chicago and New York, 1958, No. 84.
C. M. de Hauke, *Seurat et son Oeuvre,* Paris, 1961, No. 641.
R. L. Herbert, *Seurat's Drawings,* New York, 1962.

A Sunday Afternoon on the Island of La Grande Jatte (Chicago) was Seurat's most ambitious undertaking in his short life. For months, he went daily to his motif on the Seine, near Neuilly. In over thirty oil sketches and an equal number of drawings, he prepared the painting, studying segments of the terrain, single figures, and groups. Curiously enough, only this drawing and one oil sketch (John Hay Whitney Collection) show the locality complete and identical with the final work—minus figures (the oil sketch even without the dog). Probably they were done in the studio, and at a time when the painting was well advanced. Seurat perhaps wished to clarify the stage setting and to see it without the actors.

The ambience of the drawing comes surprisingly close to that in the fully staffed painting. One stands in front of an invisible barrier, behind which is the untouchable space, vibrating with an arrested motion. In the drawing there is an added note of eeriness, because of the emptiness and silence.

In its sheer graphic perfection, this page is fascinating. Seurat used a rough paper whose surface allowed a highly nuanced touch of the greasy crayon. The reader will observe the gradations from white to black. He also will notice that some shadows are not cast by factual objects, and serve only the refinement of the layout.

Vincent van Gogh
Groot-Zundert (Holland) 1853–1890 Auvers

145. *A Suburb of Paris*
1886/87
Black and colored crayon, watercolor heightened in white, traces of pen,
390 × 530 mm (15 3/8 × 20 7/8″)
Gemeente Museum, Amsterdam

BIBL. : J. B. de la Faille, *L'Oeuvre de Vincent van Gogh,* Paris-Brussels, 1928, No. 1410.
J. Rewald, *Post-Impressionism from Van Gogh to Gauguin,* New York, 1956.

When Van Gogh moved from the Netherlands to France in February 1886, he realized at once what he had to learn from Impressionism and Neo-Impressionism. Soon, he was painting in brighter colors, with a lighter touch and a more adroit layout.

However, one would not mistake this drawing for the work of a Frenchman. The industrial suburb (Clichy? Saint-Ouen?) probably reminded Van Gogh of the Borinage where, as a lay preacher, he had shared the life of the Belgian coal miners. He was deeply involved with the common man's lot, and therefore had a great admiration for Courbet and Millet. He copied many of Millet's paintings of rural life which in particular impressed him. Yet, Van Gogh's approach is not the same. To Millet, the socialist, a peasant is a member of a class. He views him with mixed respect and pity, that is, from the outside, albeit with affection. Van Gogh is without any bias, he considers the workers and farmers whom he paints as his equals; he looks at a loom or a hoe with the eyes of the man who has to use it. Not so much a social as a humane conscience is awake in him. It can be sensed in this drawing as well, although not a single person is visible.

See also Introduction, p. 31.

Vincent van Gogh

146. *Fields and Farmhouses near Arles*
1888
Pencil and reed pen, 255 × 345 mm (10 1/16 × 13 9/16″)
Gemeente Museum, Amsterdam

BIBL. : J. B. de la Faille, *op. cit.*, No. 1474.
The Complete Letters of Vincent van Gogh, New York, 1958.

Van Gogh left Paris in February 1886 and found in Provence the nature for which he was longing. "My God," he wrote to Emile Bernard, "if only I'd known this country at the age of twenty-five instead of thirty-five. At that time, my passion was for grayness or rather drabness" (Letters, II, p. 491).

In July, he did several drawings, some very large, of the Crau, the plain south of Arles, with roads crossing the diverse fields, and tiny figures walking in the sun (Letters, II, p. 610). Probably from the same month is this smaller sheet of fields with wheat and poppies in a soft wind. The location seems to be closer to Arles. The drawing is almost identical with a painting (De la Faille, No. 576), but not necessarily a preparation for it. Van Gogh considered such elaborate sheets as finished works.

Most of the Arles drawings were done with the reed pen. Van Gogh had used it occasionally in Holland, but now he found a better quality of reed and took full advantage of it. Using several pens, differently sharpened, and two shades of ink, he expressed forms and colors with a strength and subtlety that had rarely been achieved in this medium.

See also Introduction, p. 31.

Vincent van Gogh

147. *The Sower in the Rain*
      (verso: A Peasant Hoeing)
      1888/90
      Pencil, 240 × 275 mm (9 7/16 × 10 13/16″)
      Gemeente Museum, Amsterdam

BIBL. : J. B. de la Faille, *op. cit.,* No. 1551.

The wind and rain give an added pathos to the landscape. The drawing goes beyond the scope of the preceding sheet. No longer is Van Gogh concerned with the fields and cottages as such, or with the person of the sower. In the vehement strokes of the pencil, he endeavors to harness an agitation which he sees in all existence.

No doubt, the drawing betrays his desperate state of health, which, at the same time, made him uncommonly percipient. Such works herald the art of the twentieth century. Millet's *Sower* lies far behind in a less disturbed past.

Whether the sheet was done in Saint-Rémy or, according to De la Faille, at Auvers, it has the grim intensity of the master's latest creations.

See also Introduction, p. 32.

Edvard Munch
Løten (Norway) 1863–1944 Ekely (Norway)

148. *"In Us Are Worlds"*
Signed "E. Munch" and dated 1894
Pencil and black chalk, 363 × 312 mm (14 5/16 × 12 1/4")
Munch-Museet, Oslo

BIBL. : O. Benesch, *Edvard Munch,* London, 1960.
J. H. Langaard and R. Revold, *Edvard Munch,* New York, 1964.
L. Nochlin, *op. cit.,* pp. 203 ff.

The drawing brings us to the threshold of modern times. The very title indicates that this is no longer "landscape" in the former sense. As often, Munch sets the human face off against a large space as if to symbolize the tension and affinity between the inner and the outer worlds. In most cases, the face is strictly frontal, for example in *The Shriek* (painting, 1893; woodcut, 1895), where "the rhythm of the long, wavy lines seems to carry the echo of the scream into every corner of the picture, making of earth and sky one great sounding board of fear" (H. W. Janson, *History of Art*, New York, 1962, p. 509). In our sheet, Munch has turned the head into profile, as he did with that of the *Sick Girl* whom he depicted repeatedly.

It stands to reason that some of the artists who grew up in the last decades of the past century struggled a long time to find their direction. Edvard Munch was in his thirties when he turned away from the Impressionist tradition and did this symbolic drawing. How he thought and felt during those years in Paris has been related by him vividly (Nochlin).

Emil Nolde
Nolde (North Schleswig) 1867–1956 Seebüll

149. *Mooring Posts and Steam Barges in the Harbor of Hamburg,*
on a Stormy Day
C. 1910
Brush in India ink, 320×400 mm (12 5/8×15 3/4″)
Kunsthalle, Hamburg, No. 1916/127

BIBL. : W. Haftmann, Exhibition Catalogue, *German Art of the Twentieth Century,* The Museum
of Modern Art, New York, 1957, p. 34.
P. Selz, Exhibition Catalogue, *Emil Nolde,* The Museum of Modern Art, New York, 1963.

It is commonly accepted that today's easy communications draw the countries closer together—culturally at least. Yet comparing Nolde with Mondrian (plate 151), one has to admit that national dispositions remain ever divergent. In birth date, the two are only a few years apart, but the art of each denotes entirely different attitudes. Such diversity should be considered a positive value; it enriches our world.

Nolde reacts to the challenge of his time not unlike some of his German predecessors in the age of the Reformation. He states his visual-spiritual convictions in an emphatic language, that of Expressionism. His colors bespeak an intensely glowing nature, his religious paintings present ungainly and ecstatic believers.

Everything becomes fluid and dynamic in his hand and appears to be "in the making." This sheet belongs to a series of black-on-white drawings, rare in Nolde's work, and done in Hamburg. The agitated waters, the contrasting darks and lights give a harsh note to the scene, which does not look like the busy harbor in the center of a thriving city.

Lyonel Feininger
New York 1871–1956 New York

150. *Landscape with Mountains and Water*
Signed "Feininger" and dated 1936
Pen and sepia wash, 237 × 417 mm (9 3/8 × 16 1/2")
Collection Mrs. Agnes R. Claflin, New Paltz, N.Y.

BIBL.: H. Hess, *Lyonel Feininger*, London, 1961.
E. Ruhmer, *Lyonel Feininger, Zeichnungen, Aquarelle, Graphik*, Munich, 1961.

Feininger came to Germany at the age of sixteen and returned to the United States when he was sixty-five. He is now claimed by both countries. In any case, he does not share the emotional temper of some of the north European artists.

The landscape, freely invented, recalls the Rhine or a Scandinavian fjord. In spite of the picturesque setting, it is impersonal, even depersonalized. A traveler would be out of place in this spotless country, into which castle and ships are set like toys. Fittingly, all the lines, the framing ones as well as those inside, are drawn with the ruler, in varying strength and continuity. Feininger's art is less cerebral than it appears. There is a ring of music in those translucent planes and spaces which are tuned to each other with an exquisite clarity.

Feininger   1930

Piet Mondrian
Amersfoort (Holland) 1872–1944 New York

151. *Bare Tree*
Signed "P. Mondrian"
1912
Black chalk, 565×845 mm (22 1/4×33 1/4")
Gemeente Museum, The Hague, No. T 37–1957

BIBL. : P. Mondrian, *Plastic Art and Pure Plastic Art 1937 and Other Essays 1941–1943*, New York, 1945.

The huge drawing is from a time when Mondrian was still searching for a canon which eventually would be consummate abstraction. He recalls his striving in *Toward the True Vision of Reality* (1942), pp. 10, 13: "The time was around 1910 when Cubism was in its beginnings. . . . I felt that only the Cubists had discovered the right path; and, for a time, I was much influenced by them.

"Gradually I became aware that Cubism did not accept the logical consequences of its own discoveries; it was not developing abstraction towards its ultimate goal, the expression of pure reality. . . . It took me a long time to discover that particularities of form and natural color evoke subjective states of feeling, which obscure *pure reality*. . . . To create pure reality plastically, it is necessary to reduce natural forms to the *constant elements* of form and natural color to *primary color*.

"I found that the right angle is the only constant relationship, and that, through the proportions of dimensions, its constant expression can be given movement, that is, made living.

"During this period of research in Paris, I made many abstract paintings of trees, houses, plants and other objects. . . . But I felt that I still worked as an Impressionist . . . I felt that one can become less and less subjective, until the subjective no longer predominates in one's work.

"More and more I excluded from my painting all curved lines . . ."*

* Reprinted by permission of Harry Holtzman, Lyme, Conn.

Paul Klee
Münchenbuchsee (Switzerland) 1879–1940 Muralto-Locarno

152.   *"Verlassener Garten"*
Signed "Klee" and dated 1909
Pen, 235 × 215 mm (9 1/4 × 8 7/16")
Collection Mrs. Renée Ziegler, Zürich

BIBL. : W. Grohmann, *Paul Klee,* New York, 1954.
Paul Klee, Bern and Surroundings, Watercolors, and Drawings 1897–1915, Kornfeld and Klipstein, Bern, 1963.
Exhibition Catalogue, *Paul Klee,* Renée Ziegler Gallery, Zürich, 1963, No. 3.
The Diaries of Paul Klee 1898–1918, Berkeley and Los Angeles, 1964.

The page illustrates Klee at a stage prior to his esoteric imagery. The garden may have been sketched from nature, either in Bern or in Munich. The artist drew many factual sites at that time; he noted then in his diary "I am collecting forms and perspectives from nature with the ardor of a bee" (p. 238). Yet the scratches of his pen trace a poetic web that bespeaks reverie more than observation. One needs the title to read the drawing correctly. "Verlassener Garten" can mean a secluded or abandoned or neglected garden—probably the sheet conveys all three. The ambivalence of Klee's art, with logic and fancy interacting, is already present in this enticing and little-known work.

Pablo Ruiz Picasso
Born Málaga 1881

153. *Villa at Vallauris*
Dated 14.9.52
Brush in India ink, 505 × 660 mm (19 7/8 × 26″)
Present whereabouts unknown

BIBL. : C. Zervos, *Pablo Picasso, Oeuvres,* Paris, 1932—.

Nature has not been a frequent theme of Picasso. When he drew landscapes,

he did several within a short time—see Zervos, Vols. 4 and 13.

No comment is expected here. One is familiar with the artist's shorthand

writing.

Max Beckmann
Leipzig 1884–1950 New York

154.   *Southern Coast*
Signed "Beckmann" and dated '47
Pen, 247×330 mm (9 11/16×13")
Collection Mr. and Mrs. Perry Rathbone, Cambridge, Mass.

BIBL. : E. Göpel, *Max Beckmann der Zeichner*, Munich, 1954, No. 39.
M. Beckmann, *Tagebücher 1940–1950*, Munich, 1955.
P. Selz, Exhibition Catalogue, *Max Beckmann*, The Museum of Modern Art, New York, 1964.

During his ten years in Holland, where Beckmann found refuge and new friends, he created many of his most eminent works. After the end of the war, his first trip abroad, in April 1947, took him to the Côte d'Azur. His diary tells of the pleasure of seeing mountains again, of driving around the Riviera, of moving in a cosmopolitan world.

A breath of freedom can be felt in this drawing, a view from the Grande Corniche, where Beckmann stopped for a few minutes, on the way from Nice to Monte Carlo. The sheet was not drawn on the spot, however, but later in Amsterdam. Beckmann did not make such large drawings while before the motif; if anything, he took a few notations on a small piece of paper. His exceptional memory allowed him to execute the actual work at home.*

A brief comment cannot say anything relevant on Beckmann's art, which belongs to the truly great of our century. The reader who is already conversant with it will recognize it also in this oddly rudimentary and naked landscape, with the large sundisk, its domineering highways and diminutive cars—it does not quite resemble the Riviera of our experience; it alludes to deeper forces and elicits more signal connotations.

* I am grateful to Mrs. Mathilde Q. Beckmann for this information.

Mark Tobey
Born Centerville (Wisconsin) 1890

155. *Long Island Spring*
Signed "Tobey" and dated 1957
Sumi ink, 610×495 mm (24×19 1/2")
Collection Mrs. Marian Willard Johnson, New York City

BIBL. : W. C. Seitz, Exhibition Catalogue, *Mark Tobey,* The Museum of Modern Art, New York, 1962, No. 107.

Like Paul Klee, Tobey gives to his works titles which supply the key to the allusive intent. Without the caption, one would not read tree, foliage, and atmosphere into these splashes, scratches, and dots. *Long Island Spring* is a plain designation; but more often than not, the names combine a philosophical with the representational meaning. Such labels as *Without Man, Dragonade, Universal City, Canal of Cultures* add another and essential dimension.

One is allowed to ask whether the artist knows his titles beforehand, or whether they occur to him during and after the execution of a work. I have been told that, as a rule, the former is true.* Anyway, there seems to be a genuine parallelism of the visual and the mental processes.

On the series of drawings in black ink (exceptional for Tobey who relies on color), the artist wrote: ". . . it happened one day, a suggestion from a brown-black painting which I felt could be carried on in blacks. How long I had these Sumi paintings in cold storage or had the delayed-unrealized desire to paint them I don't know. It was a kind of fever, like the earth in spring, or a hurricane. Of course I can give many reasons, that they were the natural growth from my experience with the brush and Sumi ink in Japan and China, but why did I wait some twenty years before doing them?" (K. Kuh, *The Artist's Voice,* New York, 1962, p. 244).

* I am grateful to Mrs. Johnson for this information.

Henry Moore
Born Castleford, Yorkshire (England) 1898

156. *Stones in a Landscape*
Signed "Moore" and dated 36
Pen and wash, 550×375 mm (21 5/8 × 14 3/4")
Collection Mrs. William F. C. Ohly, New Barnet, England

BIBL. : *Henry Moore, Sculpture and Drawings,* ed. by D. Sylvester, London, 1957, Vol. I, p. 198.

Henry Moore's sculpture has an affinity to nature and therefore feels at home out of doors. Somehow, it connotes the formations of the earth; it respects the materials of stone or metal, and the famous holes are parts of a large and inclusive airspace.

In this drawing, the antediluvial colosses, in their diverse positions and elevations, are fitting inhabitants of the landscape. The lack of any vegetative matter enhances the grandeur of the expanse.

The little white "temples" which, at first sight, look like raisins in a big cake, add in fact a man-made dimension to that of nature.

Alberto Giacometti
Stampa (Switzerland) 1901–1966 Chur

157. *A Rocky Peak in the Alps*
Signed "Alberto Giacometti" and dated 1957
Pencil, 501×654 mm (19 3/4×25 3/4")
The Solomon R. Guggenheim Museum, New York City, No. 1481

BIBL. : J. Lord, *A Giacometti Portrait,* New York, 1964.
Exhibition Catalogue, *Alberto Giacometti,* The Museum of Modern Art, New York, 1965, No. 131.

An absorbing initiation into Giacometti has been given by James Lord, who relates the making of the portrait for which the author was sitting. Originally planned to take "an hour or two, an afternoon at most," the painting eventually took no fewer than eighteen days. Lord describes how the artist struggled day by day to achieve perfection, how he painted, then undid, then repainted the portrait several times. The book provides an insight into an artist's mental workshop such as we rarely obtain.

Probably, this mountain also did not attain its form as readily as one would believe. Giacometti may have shaped its configuration in his mind for a long time, if, as can be assumed, it is one of the summits in his native Bergell. The same as the portraits, it has a decided individuality, which is based not so much on its factual features as on the crystalline clarification achieved by the artist.

Alberto Giacometti
1957,

Graham Sutherland
Born London 1903

158. *Outcast Coal Production, Excavators Uncovering a Coal Seam*
Signed "Sutherland"
1943
Pen, chalk and watercolor, 444 × 864 mm (17 1/2 × 34″)
Imperial War Museum, London

BIBL. : D. Cooper, *The Work of Graham Sutherland,* London, 1961, No. 47.

In 1940, Sutherland was appointed an official "war artist" by the British Government. Many of the subjects assigned to him were located in Wales, as for instance this open coal mine in the mountains.

Without a commission, strip mining may not have attracted him, but it certainly grew in his hand to stature (and to a size which is immense for a drawing).

Again, here is the peculiar English knack for a narrative display that persists even in our century when subject matter *per se* has lost much of its old significance.

Alfred Manessier

Born Saint-Ouen (Somme) 1911

159. *Montagnes près d'Aups*
Signed "Manessier" and dated 59
Brush in Chinese ink, 640×985 mm (25 3/16×38 3/4")
Musée de l'Art Moderne, Paris, No. 2064D

BIBL. : O. H. Moe, "Manessier Oppdageret et Nytt Lanskap" (Manessier Discovers a New Landscape), *Kunsten Idag,* 1959, No. 4, pp. 38 ff.
Exhibition Catalogue, *Ink Drawings from Haute Provence,* Galerie de France, Paris, 1959.

Manessier spent an entire summer at the village of Moissac-Bellevue, in the department of Var, where he drew the Alpine mountains. To a man born and raised in northern France, the South was a stirring experience, as it had been to countless Europeans of the North.

Read the artist speaking of his drawings when they were exhibited in Paris: "I am amazed at the exuberance of all these drawings which now cover the walls, like major works of art, 'opuses in themselves,' when I consider that this means of expression was never, as far as I am concerned, anything but a matter of notes and jottings . . . which had long since surrendered their substance to the paintings of which, for a moment, they had provided the foundation. This new phenomenon is, undeniably, the result of a 'shock encounter' with the Midi. . . . No sooner had I arrived than I was seized by a fit of energy, not least novel in my case because it only found its outlet in drawing—in spontaneous, subtle, living lines, full of light and space, rhythms which engulfed me with their waves, wherever I turned, compelling me to consider in all seriousness this intense life, as if it were an internal tragedy, with the nerves of my hand 'connected up' like a needle on a gramophone record."

Robert Motherwell
Born Aberdeen (Washington) 1915

160. *Beside the Sea #26*
1962
Acrylic on paper, 733 × 584 mm (28 7/8 × 23″)
Collection the artist

BIBL. : Frank O'Hara, Exhibition Catalogue, *Robert Motherwell,* The Museum of Modern Art, New York, 1965, No. 63.

Although the huge sheet is done in paint, the white of the paper, the garland of the signature lend it a graphic quality that allows claiming it as a drawing of sorts.

It belongs to a series of several dozen, all called *Beside the Sea,* all suggesting heaving water and the splash of a wave, each one different. Hand and brush have taken over; one enjoys their forcefulness and accepts their function to recreate nature. But is this still landscape or, to be correct, seascape? If so, an "image made by chance"?

Again, we let the artist speak: "I don't exploit so-called 'accidents' in painting. I accept them if they seem appropriate. There is no such thing as an 'accident' really; it is a kind of casualness: it happened so let it be, so to speak. One doesn't want a picture to look 'made' like an automobile or a loaf of bread in waxed paper. Precision belongs to the world of machinery— which has its own forms of the beautiful. . . . But machinery created with brush and paint is ridiculous . . . I agree with Renoir, who loved everything hand-made" (O'Hara, p. 54).

How far away from the old standards has history led us! To where? The future will tell.

Selected Bibliography

Clark, Kenneth M. *Landscape Painting*. New York: Scribner's, 1950.

Friedländer, Max J. *Landscape, Portrait, Still-Life*. New York: Schocken, 1963, pp. 11 ff.

Gombrich, E. H. "Renaissance Artistic Theory and the Development of Landscape Painting." *Gazette des Beaux-Arts,* Paris, 1953, pp. 335 ff.

Hasselt, C. van. *Dessins de Paysagistes Hollandais du XVIIe Siècle de la Collection Particulière conservée à l'Institut Néerlandais de Paris*. Exhibition Catalogue, Brussels, Rotterdam, Paris, and Bern, 1968/69.

Knab, E. *Claude Lorrain und die Meister der Römischen Landschaft im XVII. Jahrhundert.* Exhibition Catalogue, Albertina, Vienna, 1964/65.

L'Ideale Classico del Seicento in Italia e la Pittura di Paesaggio. Exhibition Catalogue, Bologna, 1962.

Mongan, Agnes, ed. *One Hundred Master Drawings*. Cambridge: Harvard University Press, 1949 (See in particular "Glossary of Materials" by W. Ames, pp. 205 ff.).

Mongan, Agnes. "European Landscape Drawing 1400–1900; a Brief Survey." *Daedalus,* Boston, 1963, pp. 581 ff.

Stechow, Wolfgang. *Dutch Landscape Painting of the Seventeenth Century*. London: Phaidon, 1966.

Turner, A. R. *The Vision of Landscape in Renaissance Italy*. Princeton: Princeton University Press, 1966.

Watrous, James. *The Craft of Old Master Drawings*. Madison: University of Wisconsin Press, 1957.

Index of Artists

Photo Credits

The author and publisher wish to thank the museums and private collectors for permitting the reproduction in black-and-white of drawings in their collections. Photographs have been supplied by the owners of the works of art except for the following, whose courtesy is gratefully acknowledged:

Archives Photographiques, Paris: 13, 19, 72, 103, 107; Bulloz, Paris: 128; Clements, Geoffrey, New York: 155; Courtauld Institute of Art, London: 9, 75, 76, 89, 90; Dingjan, A., The Hague: 86; Fleming, R. B. and Co., Ltd., London: 113; Frequin, A., The Hague: 10, 77, 99; Galerie Louise Leiris, Paris: 153; Giraudon, Paris: 59; Grünert, Peter, Zurich: 152; Guggenheim Museum, New York: 160; Josse, Hubert, Paris: 126; Meriden Gravure Co., Meriden, Conn.: 50; Newbery, Sydney, London: 120; Photo Studios Ltd., London: 114; Resseguié, Montauban: 122; Royal Museum, Copenhagen: 93; Schiff, John, New York: 138; Service de Documentation Photographique, Paris: 1, 11, 51, 52, 54, 121, 159; Spearman, George, Windsor, England: 5, 6, 7, 56, 112; Stearn and Sons, Ltd., Cambridge, England: 110; University Press, Oxford: 47.

RENNER LEARNING RESOURCES CENTER
ELGIN COMMUNITY COLLEGE
ELGIN, ILLINOIS